BLOOD STAINS & BALLGOWNS

MY LIFE AS A CRIME SCENE CLEANER

DONNA NAYLER

National Library of Australia Cataloguing-in-Publication entry (pbk)

Creator:	Nayler, Donna, author.
Title:	Bloodstains and Ball Gowns / Donna Nayler.
ISBN:	978-1-925388-27-5 (paperback) 978-1-925388-28-2 (eBook)
Subjects:	Nayler, Donna. Crime scenes Anecdotes. Crime scenes Cleaning.

Dewey Number: 363.25

Published by Donna Nayler and InHouse Publishing
www.inhousepublishing.com.au

Printed using Envirocare paper

Dedication

The dedication of this book is split many ways.

To Mum and Dad

To Lisa

To Rob, Jerry and Kyle

To Ocean and InHouse Publishing

To Jade and Mark

To Lynn

To all those who I met along the way behind the blue and white chequered tape.

Most importantly those who lives were lost and reborn in the pages, and to all of you who have listened to me, inspired me and believed in me.

Thank you

Contents

Crime Scene Cleaner

Everybody has a story. This is mine. What makes me think my story is worth telling?

I speak for the dead, and for what the dead have left behind.

When we are young, our teachers and parents ask the age-old question, "What do you want to be when you grow up?"

'Crime scene cleaner' isn't the usual answer.

I grew up amid the sparkling lights of Australia's Gold Coast, and my friends were all in sales or hairdressing, girls stuck in girly jobs. A bit of a rebel, I skipped school regularly until I convinced my parents I had made my decision in life. I was going to live in society and earn a wage rather than attend my final year of schooling.

My euphoric rush of instant adulthood was short lived. I was told to get a job and get used to the real world.

I'm still trying to get used to the real world.

I began hairdressing at seventeen, but by the age of twenty-five, I was tired of pretending I cared about what was going on in my clients' lives, tired of their first-world problems. Venting to the unlucky hairdresser must be cheaper than going to a shrink.

I'd always been intrigued and fascinated by death services, eager to delve into the darkness, while at the same time it freaked me out. I've always believed in the supernatural and wondered what happens after your heart stops ticking.

What is left in the silent moments after the grim reaper has come and gone?

It was finally the TV show 'Crime Investigation' that triggered me to look into the industry that so fascinated me. My dad was behind my questionable idea to clean crime scenes, and so my journey began. If there is one thing I am grateful for, it is my parents' unwavering love and support.

I researched extensively, but it was a tight-lipped industry. Only a handful of companies offered this service, and most of them were regular house cleaners who did it on the side to earn a few extra dollars. And I was to learn that it did pay extremely well. It was like a secret society.

This didn't deter me. My parents remained supportive. My friends told me to go for it, although I could tell they thought I was mad.

Life is for the living, even if it requires mopping up the dead.

I only wanted to learn from the best, and so it was that I came across Australia's biggest company. I was around at my friend's house drinking tea and working up the courage to call. If they say no, I'll cry, I thought. I called the number and started talking at a hundred miles an hour. They were based in Cairns although they worked Australia-wide. As fate would have it, they were in Surfers Paradise cleaning up a drug lab the police had found in one of the hotels.

They invited me up for an interview within the hour.

"This is it!" I screamed.

Wearing my friend's dress, stockings and heels, all black of course, I jumped in my car and flew up the highway to the unknown.

Walking into the foyer of the well-known Gold Coast hotel, my heels clacking on the polished floor, I looked over at reception to see a man standing at the counter wearing a black-and-white checked shirt. He was deep in conversation with the concierge. I waited for them to finish talking and then politely asked the man if he was the person I had come to see.

He was a gentle looking man of strong build, with dark hair and a friendly smile. Containing my excitement and sheer terror, I shook the hand he offered in greeting as he smiled and introduced himself.

"Let's go up." He gestured to follow him to the lift.

As we were alone in the lift, he told me that the drug lab was on the same floor as they were staying. The lab had been discovered because the housemaid had passed out from the chemical haze in the air. Everyone from the floor had been evacuated.

"Did the guests ask why?" I asked, my mouth so dry I could barely get the words out.

"Their rooms were all upgraded," he said, "so no one complained."

This is so exciting, I thought, although I simply smiled and nodded.

We went up to a floor that I can't tell you, in a hotel I can't name. I can't tell anyone. I am sworn to secrecy about all the places I visit in the course of my work. Names and addresses are not public knowledge, unless the media get their hands on the story, that is.

The lift doors opened and we turned right down the corridor.

A door at the end of the corridor was open. He told me it was the room they were staying in.

We approached the drug lab room and I saw that it was dark inside. Sheets covered the windows, allowing neither the light nor the outside world in. I looked around and said nothing for a few moments, taking it all in. It was bare; no carpets, no bed, no furniture. It didn't look like a hotel room at all. He explained that all the contents of the room were contaminated and had been removed. They were very lucky, he said, that the air conditioning was contained to each room and not ducted. Otherwise, the entire hotel would have had to be evacuated. I had heard of drug labs being found in hotel rooms before but I'd never realised the damage they caused.

"It's safe now," he said, "but we've been here a week already. We're almost finished."

We continued down the corridor to the end room and went inside. This room was furnished normally. I sat down and at that moment, another man came through the door. He looked worn out from the day's work, but still had an air of energy and excitement about him. He was slightly taller, with sandy hair. He smiled at me, introduced himself and threw himself down on the lounge, kicking his feet in the air. I was sitting at a small round table with two chairs on either side. There was paperwork covering the tabletop and I was trying hard not to read it. The two men were very welcoming and they talked about the operation, asking me for my thoughts from time to time. They seemed impressed with me, even though I am a five-foot-nothing blonde hairdresser. I had the magic inside me, the drive. That fire in my belly pushed me in the right direction.

I felt like part of the team already, a secret society. I knew what no one else outside of this room did.

The drug cooks had taken off when the housemaid had collapsed, but the police knew they would eventually be lulled into complacence and return to collect the two-hundred-dollar bond from the hotel. Five unmarked police cars waited outside for their return.

The interview wound down after about an hour, and I'll never forget when they said, "Pack your bags and wait for a call." It was hard not to jump over the table in excitement.

The true events in this book tell the story about what can go horribly wrong in life, love and behind the chequered police tape.

We All Love a Bad Boy

I never thought the day would come.

"Want to come see another drug lab?" He said down the phone.

Without hesitation, I took the first flight out of the Gold Coast and headed to Rockhampton.

I was nervous, excited and scared all at the same time.

I had no idea what I would have to do or what I would see. Would I be able to handle it?

I pictured it to be like a scene out of the movie 'Wonderland'. Drug-hazed rooms with holes in the walls and bodies that had been beaten to death, lying naked on the beds.

How wrong I was.

I arrived in Rockhampton late in the afternoon, on a hot, humid day. We were staying at a motel beside the highway. Our view was of dried grass and withered trees. The noise of trucks booming by went right through me. The motel owner showed me to my room. Standing in the corner was a toolbox on wheels, bigger than my suitcase, half the size of me in fact. I unpacked and went out the front to see the rest of the team. My new boss beamed at me, asking if I had seen my present. I nodded shyly.

"Come on, I'll show you all your gear," he said, walking into my room and wheeling the toolbox over.

I was in awe of the number of drawers filled with the unusual things I would need. It was the best gift I could ever have dreamed of. I am ready to become a crime scene cleaner, I thought.

The next morning, wearing my new uniform – white singlet with professional black-and-navy-blue button-up shirt with the company name across the back, and hat to match, I looked the part. It felt like my first day at school and I couldn't wipe the grin off my face.

It wouldn't be long before that grin was gone, although the fire would always burn inside me.

On the car ride to the site, it hit me; this was the first day of my secret life. Only two workers normally attended a job and I felt privileged to be allowed to come along for the ride. They laughed and joked and helped me feel at ease and to look forward to my day ahead, even though I might have felt nervous because I was on trial.

During the ride, they filled me in on what I would be facing at the end of the gravel road and what the 'stage one' clean-up had entailed. They had started the job a week before and were waiting for the payee to confirm commencement of 'stage two', which was where I came in.

They told me that the owner of the house, a known member of a notorious outlawed motorcycle gang, had been on the run since the police had found his drug lab and extensive gun collection inside the property, although later, we were told by the police he was away working in the mines. I was confused as to how someone could be caught with guns and a drug lab and not be incarcerated instantly. The only reason he had been caught was because he had missed his repayments on the property for some months, therefore forfeiting it to the bank, who upon changing the locks and entering were shocked at what they found inside.

Gases produced by the cooking of chemicals that make up illegal party drugs will knock you out as effectively as being in the ring with Mohammed Ali.

When the crime scene clean-up team had turned up the first time to inspect the property, the police had been there to escort them, because a sawn-off shotgun was reportedly missing. It was a concern that they had known about the shotgun in the first place and taken no action. When the police left and my two colleagues were left alone, the fugitive had come running from the bushes, screaming and yelling at them. My co-worker, who is an amazing man, stood up to him and calmed him down. He explained what they were doing there and that they had nothing to do with the investigation process, just the clean-up to ensure the safety of the child and those around him, including himself. My co-workers are the most dedicated and enthusiastic people I have ever known and to this day, I still love them.

The man calmed down and left, albeit temporarily. The police weren't far away and he was a wanted man. He wasn't stupid.

The bank had changed the locks to stop the owner getting inside. Touché to the bikie, in the middle of the night he changed the locks again and barricaded himself inside with the sawn-off shotgun. Nobody dared demand to be let in. During the day, he disappeared again. The team needed to get rid of his belongings, including a Dodge Viper and a custom designed Harley Davidson in the garage attached to the house, to prevent him from coming back.

I'll admit I was nervous, yet what normal nine-to-five worker gets this much excitement in an office? Secretly, I was very excited about the experiences to come. Every girl loves a bad boy, a leather jacket and a motorcycle. Think Marlon Brando, Grease and The Fonz. However, bad in the days of these icons wasn't the same as what bad is now. When bad becomes ugly, that's a turn-off, and bad becomes ugly when a guy is a drug cook who sticks needles in his arms to get high and wonders why he is shunned by society. He thinks he is above the law.

We drove down the pebble-stone driveway leading to a shed behind a brick house in matching tones. It was a barn style shed standing alone in an open field with overgrown grass, and the shed was sealed off with the familiar blue and white chequered police tape. A rusty chicken wire fence encircled the property.

Leaving the vehicle, I followed my colleagues to the front door so they could unload the car and begin setting up the equipment. With my new toolbox in tow, I entered the home. It looked to be only a couple of years old, with large bedrooms off each side of the long corridor.

It was hard labour, with every square inch of the house having to be washed clean. If we missed any part, it would cost my boss thousands of dollars to have the site retested. Unlike blood or brain, the drug residue was invisible. The work was tedious at times, but I had to be focused. My career depended on it.

My excitement rose when I found shotgun pellets, .22-calibre rounds, along with parts of the meth lab and multiple syringes. In his bedroom alone, there were a hundred and sixty unprotected needles. All the carpets in the house and any porous material had already been removed. I learned that paint is a porous substance that holds chemical residue.

The five bedrooms were empty, with bare concrete floors. The house echoed. It was an eerie feeling being in this house that had once been full of life, used as a seedy drug den with endless parties.

In the back shed, a disturbing array of chemicals was displayed on the manmade wooden bench. If the people who took these substances saw them sitting on a dirty shelf in a biker's shed, they might think twice about what they put into their bodies.

The most sickening part was that one of his girlfriends stayed over regularly. She had a child who always accompanied her whenever she was summoned over for a booty call. My colleagues knew a child had been there from the cot and the toys scattered everywhere. Who knew if the baby had ever crawled over the unprotected needles, or along the carpet saturated in chemicals from the lab set up in the kitchen, or breathed in the fumes swirling in the air from cooking the drugs on the stovetop.

During stage one, my colleagues told me they used to go for a drink at the pub to wind down after work. It was amazing what they found out at the local watering hole. People love to gossip. The topic of conversation in between swigs of beer and slurring of words was the activity surrounding the biker's home. The drunken men would all put their two cents' worth in. They did manage to sort out the truth from the lies.

I enjoyed going to work every day and developed a great friendship with my co-workers. Two days into the job, the work phone rang and I could hear muffled shouting coming through the speaker. My boss's face dropped. The accused had sent someone up for a sticky beak and that person had got our number from our sign-written truck. He was mad that we were back. My stomach dropped the same as if I'd been on a rollercoaster.

He paced back and forth after hanging up. He told us that the biker knew how many of us were at his house, what time we arrived each day, and what time we left.

"I'll break your legs!" he'd said.

Having someone want to break your legs was preferable to what I was about to experience.

Blah blah blah. I wasn't scared. I knew many boys just like him on the Gold Coast. All talk, no go. Their tattoos make them appear tougher than they are. My boss explained again to the biker why we were there, and that we didn't work for the police. The biker was afraid that we would incriminate him more. He was told that we were there to make his house safe again. We had heard from the local pub that his father was buying the house back off the bank. He brought to his attention again about the child's safety and told him he could watch what we were doing if he wanted to. Too far, I thought to myself. By the end of the phone call, he had calmed down. Several more times, he rang back to find out what was happening.

By moving his meth lab into the kitchen, the biker had contaminated all the insulation in the ceiling above, and so to make the house safe, all the insulation had to be removed. These chemicals cause skin irritation, and breathing them in can cause respiratory damage and in severe cases, respiratory failure resulting in death. I was told that if I felt light-headed and my heart started racing, I needed to remove myself from the situation.

The humidity in Rockhampton is at a hundred percent in the middle of summer. I was standing with my colleagues beneath the manhole, the three of us debating who would be the unlucky soul to squeeze up through the manhole into the sweltering heat of the ceiling. I was wearing a white suit toggled tight up under my chin, latex gloves and a full face mask, trying to prepare myself for the thought of going up into the roof for the rest of the day and possibly all the next day. My body was already dripping with sweat from the intense heat inside my suit, and I wasn't even in the double insulated roof yet, where the toxic gases had been sucked through the kitchen exhaust fan and absorbed by the pale yellow, fibrous, itchy insulation.

There was only one way to get insulation out: by hand.

If I was going to prove myself worthy, that moment was now. Being the smallest and the newest, I pulled the short straw. I had never been into a ceiling before. All I kept thinking about were snakes. I hate snakes. They make my skin crawl. Australia has the five most deadly snakes in the world all living in our back yard. The Taipan is without a doubt the most deadly. The Taipan prefers warm climates. The further north you travel, like Rockhampton for example, the more prominent they become. To a cold-blooded reptile, there is no better place than the dark, warm protection of a ceiling.

We were hoping that the roofing was metal sheeting, as cyclones are common in a tropical climate and tiles peel away like the skin of a banana when one hits. That way, we would be able to remove a couple of sheets to allow air and light inside, reducing the fear factor. Unfortunately for me, the roof was tiled and so my journey into the darkness began.

I began peeling the insulation away at the opening of the manhole. It was like stale fairy floss. I kept my feet firmly on the ladder to reassure myself I was still in touch with the outside world. My colleague and I took turns. Once the insulation was removed from the easiest section, we began venturing into the darkness. We had to balance like gymnasts on the crossbeams at diminishing angles as they reached the corners of the house. Then I stopped dead at a long black shape that lay ahead. If I scream, no one will hear me in the mask, I thought. I crept closer, fear engulfing me, but the closer I got, the more the fire in my belly drove me forward. Electrical tape. You've got to be kidding me. A nervous laugh escaped my lips.

This joyous task lasted for three days. Once we had removed all the insulation, we had to spray a sealant along the base, inside the roof, and across every beam in that dark hole of hell they call a ceiling. No matter how much gore I see in my life, nothing sends a shiver down my spine more than the thought of that dark hole covered in yellow fairy floss.

Once that task was complete, we continued cleaning the rest of the house. The days were long and the work hard, but I loved almost every minute of it.

One day, when we were eating our packed lunches under the veranda, we were greeted by a voice oozing with cockiness. The man was an ex-policeman who owned a crime scene cleaning company in a different state. He displayed faded old tattoos on his upper arms and he smoked like a chimney. He had come to take the final swabs from the house and shed to make sure we had completed the work to expectations. My boss had told me they had never had a call-back. I was hoping I had done them proud. The man was pleasant at first but he then became creepier and creepier towards me, making my skin crawl more than the thought of snakes did. He made crude comments when I stayed close by him, only because I was interested in his work, not in him.

He finished with, "Make sure when you're down my way you look me up."

I scrunched my face up in disgust and walked away as he left in a billow of smoke. I told my colleagues in the politest way possible what I thought of him. I was new, but I wasn't going to put up with that crap. They supported me and even went as far as to look for another avenue to get the place tested. He was the best in town, and they were the best company. They needed him, and I was ok with that. Nothing was going to get in my way.

Our work wound down and I returned home, excited about what lay ahead, and waiting for my phone to ring.

Greed and Gluttony

Two weeks went by and I was itching to get amongst it again. My boss would soon be flying down to give me the necessary training. We were going to set up mock scenarios so that I could learn the techniques. When the phone rang, I jumped up to answer it and listened intently to what he said. My mind started racing. What will I see? Will the body be there? Will there be blood all over the walls?

He picked me up in the truck, and I caught myself smiling nervously in the side mirror as I got in.

We drove to the inner suburbs of Brisbane City, passing old fibro houses that had stood there for decades. We stopped outside one such home. The gates were rusty, with Singapore daisies reaching for the sun, twisting along the suffocated iron bars. Like all the other houses in the street, peeling white paint hung off the wooden panelling nailed to the front of the fibro.

A woman was standing in the driveway that was overgrown with weeds. She was a short Asian lady, skinny, with short dark hair cut into a blunt bob that framed her protruding jawline. She wore pressed white pants and a white Ralph Lauren polo. In contrast to the decay around her, gold dripped from around her neck and diamonds sparkled on her fingers.

She introduced herself and I listened as my boss asked questions. I had the paperwork in my sweaty, nervous hands, unsure of what I was to do next and what I would see.

She began to tell us that the deceased was a twenty-something-year-old-boy, who had died from natural causes in the room he rented from her. He had been in there for four days before his locked bedroom door was broken down and his lifeless body was found slumped on the wooden floor next to his bed.

At the bottom of the stairs, we put on our protective clothing. I was holding the camera to take the before, during and after photos. We always do this in case the insurance companies need proof for their records, and most importantly to prove what we did in the hours we spent there.

Walking up the wooden stairs, we were careful not to fall through the holes caused by the constant traffic of many years. This house looked as old as the first fleet.

At the top of the stairs, we entered a small sunroom. A lone incense burner sat in the centre of the room. The room was hot from the sun coming in through the mould-covered windows. The place was filthy. I was glad I was protected from head to toe. For a moment, thoughts of the dead boy were eclipsed by the mess in the house. This wasn't a home, it was a hovel.

The owner was telling my boss that the deceased had lived with two other girls. They had not realised he was missing for four days and his door was locked from the inside. How did these girls not notice anything unusual? Eventually, when they realised something wasn't right, they called the owner to complain about a foul smell oozing from the room with the locked door.

The world is often a lonely, self-absorbed place.

Along the corridor, I noticed more incense burners lining the wall. Masking the smell. The mixture of the floral scent and the smell of death made my stomach turn.

My mind was racing as I walked further into the filth. I was wearing a mask with Vicks VapoRub under my nose to detract from the smell. Vicks is my best friend, yet when I'm not working, I can't stand the smell of it.

The stench of what appeared to be rotting food increased as we moved further inside the house. Is this what a dead body smells like? I wondered.

Walking past the first bedroom on the right, I noticed that the door was open and I could hear noises coming from inside. One of the occupants had moved out because of the smell she could no longer stomach, yet another still lived there. To my disgust, she was sitting on a mattress pushed up against the back wall, surrounded by piles of dirty clothes and food scraps, in the room next door to where the boy had died. She was talking to someone on the phone, laughing and joking as she swigged out of a two-litre coke bottle, oblivious to the white-suited strangers in her abode.

As we finally entered the room that had once been the boy's retreat, and where he had spent his last moments, the words of the owner of the property ran through my mind again. He was only twenty years old. He died of natural causes.

This did not seem normal and I was suspicious, as in the room, nothing seemed out of the ordinary. Or so it seemed until the weak smell of bleach rushed up into my airways. I could tell someone had tried to clean up before we arrived, but we were there just to do our job, not to be the detectives.

We moved the shabby solid wooden bed frame over to inspect where most people would miss, and there it was. Blood underneath the bed and in the drawers attached to the frame. One of the drawers was slightly ajar, evidence that items had been taken out. There wasn't a lot of blood, a cup full at the most. Later in my career, I would see much more of it, but now, I stared down at the blood not breaking my gaze, as it was so foreign to me that I couldn't look away. It made my stomach turn, but I was fascinated. I pictured him lying on the floor. Lifeless, helpless, dying. The floor comprised wooden floorboards, with tiny gaps in between each board. There was a noticeably larger pooling of blood in between two of the boards. My boss was giving me a step-by-step guide on how to clean and what steps to take. He motioned me to follow him, and we walked back down the old stairs, past a rusty push bike and old furniture down the side of the house, and around the back, until we came to an opening where we could walk under the house to inspect.

It was hard to establish which area was beneath his room. I raced back up the stairs, making sure I didn't fall through the holes on the stairway, and lightly banged on the floor near the pooling blood. I went back down to where my boss was standing with a torch shining up onto two boards. There it was: a lot more blood, along the cracks between the floorboards and under the house.

"These floorboards will need to come up if we can't get rid of the blood," he said.

Cut the floor out. That would be cool! I thought.

Back inside, I could still hear the sloth flatmate sitting on her phone in her room. She was talking to a man, inviting him over to hang out in the house where her flatmate had died a few days earlier, and where forensic cleaners were still mopping up his bodily fluids. I could tell from the phone conversation that he had never been to the house before, as she was giving him directions.

We got our gear set up to begin the clean. I went into the kitchen for hot water, under instruction to dilute the chemicals we had brought with us to break down bodily fluids. The kitchen was as bad as the rest of the house. The smell of the deceased was masked by the smell of rotten food. I filled a bucket with water and went back to the room to begin my first clean-up after a death: removing the blood and contaminated items by hand, using a solution to dissolve the enzymes and hazardous waste, disinfecting after to remove bacteria and neutralise the area. Even though the blood was pooled in a contained area, we repeated this process throughout the room, ensuring a safe environment. During this time, I kept thinking I just wanted out of this hellhole.

When we were only about halfway through the clean-up, the owner called out to us. She was asking us to hide under the house, mumbling something about bringing a possible tenant through to rent out the room across the hall from where we were working. It was bizarre. We tried to explain to her that the girl in the room next door shouldn't still be there, let alone someone new to rent another room. Clearly, greed is a strong motivator.

We got nowhere with her and so had no choice but to hide under the house like two naughty children. It was ridiculous. We saw the feet of the unknowing possible renters as they walked up the stairs. They were there for less than five minutes.

When we finished, the room was sparkling clean and the smell of the boy's decomposing body was gone. The smell of rotting food and filth, however, was still strong in the air, but that was not what we had been hired to do. I'd rather have put a bulldozer through the place.

As we left, the owner asked us when it would be safe to rent the boy's room out again. I was disgusted but I remained silent.

Walking back down the staircase, we passed a boy. The date had arrived. I shook my head and put on my dark sunglasses.

As I was driven home, my mind ticked over.

What a sad way to die. Alone, forgotten in death. What happened to him? I wondered. Did he just die of natural causes, as the property owner had told us? All I knew for sure was that he was now at peace now. Dead men tell no tales.

Blood is Thicker Than Water

I pulled up outside a suburban North Brisbane home. A woman was standing on the footpath outside the home waiting for me. She was the occupant of the home and my point of contact to gain entry into the property. Like everyone else who first sees me on a job, she was shocked. A five-foot-nothing fifty-kilogram blonde is not what most people envision when they call a crime scene cleaner.

This was my first solo crime scene and my first murder.

I introduced myself and asked the usual question. "Could you please give me a brief run-down of what happened?"

When I learned the circumstances surrounding what had happened, I didn't know how anyone could have coped. This house had been her home, with other family members. Sadly and violently, a relative of hers had killed his nephew with the blade of a knife driven right through his heart. This family was poor and not only had a funeral to pay for but court fees for the uncle also.

I was terrified about going inside. Human instinct. Someone had been killed inside these walls. They had lost their life at someone else's hand. That is enough to send a shiver up anyone's spine. I put on a brave face. I had to show confidence and professionalism. No matter how I felt on the inside, this wasn't about me.

To this day, I relive every detail of that moment. I hate the dark, the unknown, the suspense, and I was about to face my fear of the unknown mixed with moments of anxiety as I prepared to enter the home.

Two white bed sheets had been hung between the walls of the hall that led into the entrance of the kitchen, blocking my view as to what lay ahead and behind the makeshift curtain.

I pulled them aside.

There was a dark patch of dried blood in the middle of the dining room floor, a metre in width. A blue dye seemed to have been splashed everywhere: over the walls, floor, cupboards, and fridge. Blood was even on the brand-new pool table and blood splatter was visible underneath it.

I rang my boss to ask him what the blue dye was, and he sighed and said it was amido acid and sometimes used by forensic experts to detect blood present with hidden or invisible fingerprints. It stains the proteins in the blood a blue-black colour. Because of its staining property, it made our job harder. It was also difficult to distinguish it from blood and therefore to know what cleaning products would be most effective.

Everyone who had entered the home after the attack had walked the amido acid into the carpets, creating blue shoe prints throughout the home.

The woman who had greeted me when I first arrived on the scene stayed close to me the whole time I was there. Her eyes were red from crying. I wondered what relationship she had to the deceased, but she soon told me it was her nephew's blood I was cleaning up. The killer, her cousin, was his uncle.

I told her that she could help me after I had got rid of the blood, as there was cleaning that could be done by a regular house cleaner after I had completed my job and removed the contaminated source. She could assist and restore the place to a vision of calm and peace, putting items back where they belonged as if nothing had happened.

A trail of blood began in the garage, which had been converted into an entertaining room. A table covered with a tablecloth and laden with empty bottles of Jack Daniels stood in one corner of the room. An incomplete deck of cards was scattered on the table, the rest fallen to the floor. The blood continued into the dining room, past glass sliding doors, leading towards a pool of blood that had turned dark, indicating it had been there for some time. Bloody footprints led down the hallway, which was tarnished with the same blue stains and knife marks into the Gyprock. Sprays of arterial blood covered the wall between the patches of blue.

After the dining room, we entered the laundry. It too was covered in blood and the worst affected areas by the haunting blue amido acid. The old porous laundry tub was stained so badly with it that it would have to be replaced, but the washing machine, which stood open, showing blood-soaked clothes inside waiting to be washed, would be easily wiped off. Large drops of blood lay on the floor at the base of the washing machine.

The accused had had a shower before police arrived, and the bloody water that had run from his body was pooled around the drain in the shower.

In the main bedroom, furniture was strewn around the room and there were speckles of blood on the bedroom door. The blood patterns were so unusual that I couldn't piece together in what order the events had happened. Then again, I was just a rookie, but from what I'd been told and what I could see, it seemed that the evening had started in the entertainment room with drinks flowing and card games, and then a fight had broken out. The victim had died in the same room, on the floor next to the pool table, and the weapon had been a knife from the top drawer of the kitchen. It appeared that the deceased had fought for his life, which would explain the spotting of blood down the hallway. The knife damage in the Gyprock indicated that the accused had lashed out angrily after leaving the murder scene.

My preferred solution rather than cleaning the floor coverings was to rip them up. However, the house was a rental and the owners didn't have the necessary insurance to cover unforeseen death on the property.

This kind of insurance exists, but it's never mentioned when you purchase a home. It's a taboo subject, like everything else in society that doesn't have a happy fairy tale ending. It gets forgotten, like the souls who die on the floors.

Because they didn't have the correct insurance, the owners had to pay for the crime scene cleaning, along with lawyer costs for the uncle and funeral costs for the nephew. Money was going to be scarce for a while, the woman told me with tears in her eyes. She asked if she could help me clean to keep the costs down. How could I say no?

The woman started helping me and as we were working on our hands and knees, we were startled by a knock at the door. The woman jumped up and raced to the front door. I peered around the corner, wondering who it could be. All the neighbours knew what had happened. They had all been woken by the loud noises from the fight and then blinded by the blue and red flashing lights and sirens. They wouldn't come over to see what was going on, surely? I saw another woman. She was broad and tall, with curly hair pulled roughly up on top of her head. She had a pretty face that was wet from tears streaming down her cheeks. The owner grabbed her by the arm and led her down to the main bedroom at the other end of the house. She closed the door and came back to me, telling me that the woman was the wife of the accused and the aunty of the deceased. Out of everyone, she was the most affected by this tragedy. Not only had she lost a nephew, she was going to lose her husband to manslaughter. Ten to twenty years is a long time. One moment can change the rest of your life forever.

The woman came out of the bedroom and stood beside us. She found it difficult to look at me. I smiled kindly and continued cleaning. The owner said suddenly that when all the blood was gone she would continue cleaning the blue marks on her own. One of the toughest things I had to ask so early in my career was for her to put it in writing so that I was covered. After all, this was business. The house still wasn't back to the condition it was in before that fateful night. It was hazard free, but the blue dye would be a memory trigger of a horrendous night.

I will never know the full story of what happened. There were a few others in the house that night, but blood is thicker than water so the truth may never be told.

I got in my car and called my family, to tell them I loved them. I have done it every day since.

A Fine Line Between Love and Hate

You know it's not going to be pretty when even the police inform you that the scene is horrific.

I was very nervous the morning of the job.

We had been called to another murder, this time south of the border in Ballina, in a housing commission estate for the Aboriginal community. As it was a government-owned property, we first needed to be inducted into the site.

We pulled up in front of the house to a scene I had seen many times before by now. Sheets and doona covers shielded the windows to prevent the outside world from looking in.

Two police cars were doing continuous circles of the surrounding streets.

A white Ute was parked out the front and a man in uniform was standing at the front door. He was slightly balding, with broad shoulders and a blank look on his face. He was an employee from a government department that helps those needing housing assistance. Today he appeared to be well outside of his comfort zone, looking at us with a blank empty stare as he watched us leave our vehicle. We approached him and shook his hand, which was trembling.

He had paperwork in his other hand in a manila folder. "If you feel unsafe at any time," he said, "I want you to call the police and leave." I wondered what he meant.

As we reached the front door, we saw it was smeared with a bloody handprint. Here we go.

Walking in and pushing the door aside, I led the way. A large fish tank stood against the right-hand side wall, and in the corner there was an empty Wild Turkey bottle surrounded by playing cards. They were the first signs of the night before and the beginning of the end. In the lounge room, blood had dripped from three holes in the walls that appeared to have been made by a head. They were too big and high up to have been made by a fist. The dripping blood had stained the white paint red. One of the holes was smeared and smudged with blood where someone had tried to wipe it away. This was the first of many signs of domestic violence.

We walked into the kitchen, where there was a black rubbish bag swarming with maggots. The smell made me feel sick, but the sight I was about to see when I turned my head to the left to look down the hallway is something that now haunts me forever. The best way I can describe it is, imagine if you got five litres of red paint and threw it down the hallway, smearing your hands along it.

Was this from being beaten to death, as we had been told by the gentleman who was now three paces behind us? It was worse than the stabbing scene I had been to a week before. Every room had blood throughout. The walls, floors, door frames, ceilings, even the overhead fans were covered with blood. The trail of blood kept leading towards the main bedroom. I braced myself as I walked in there. My first thought was, 'that poor girl'. I stood in horror and shook my head silently. The wooden bed frame in the main bedroom was smashed to pieces, and the wall next to the bed had another gaping hole made by her head. The blood had soaked right through the carpet and underlay to the concrete floor. The hole where her head had been pushed through had blood on the Gyprock on the other side of the wall. Fragments of her skull were visible in the heavy patches of blood.

We began stage one of the job, removing her blood and gathering valuables and belongings for the families, packing away his and her things into boxes, memories their families might or might not want to salvage. To add to our pressure, the family of the deceased girl was due to arrive the next day to collect her belongings. I began erasing the signs of the night before at the front door, beginning with the bloody handprint, and then moved into the lounge room. Reaching the hole in the Gyprock, I stood in front of it and leaned forward. The girl had been my height. Shivers ran down my spine. She had only died the night before. Once I'd finished cleaning the lounge room, I moved into the kitchen with its blue lino floor and matching cupboard doors. All had flecks of blood on them and now, I could put a face to the horror. Photos on the fridge of a couple smiled at me. I was yet to know who the killer was, but I had a feeling he was smiling down at me. I'll never forget that face; how I wish I could.

I try not to judge in this line of work. I don't know anything about the people's lives or situations. My parents always told me that if anyone you love hurts you, you must leave them and live your life without them. I just can't get the thought out of my head how anyone could have such hatred and anger towards someone they love and inflict such pain on them.

One of the lasting effects this job has had on me is that during Halloween, I don't find costumes covered in blood or bloody handprints funny anymore. I still dream of things I thought were buried deep in my mind. My dreams are probably similar to his as he sits in his jail cell. I see what he last saw.

His teenage sister had also lived in the house, and in her bedroom, her clothes, like most teenagers', were strewn all over the floor. When I met the sister, I had to explain to her that most of her belongings had had to be thrown out. I saved what I could from inside cupboards and her dresser drawers.

I felt the murdered woman's pain in every room.

The bathroom, toilet and spare bedroom, used as a storage room, were no different from the rest of the house.

When we had been there less than an hour, I was out the front disposing of bottles and broken furniture into the skip bin when a car pulled up on the front lawn and three Aboriginal women jumped out screaming at me, wanting to know what the hell I was doing. I puffed my chest out authoritatively and realised this was what the man had meant during our briefing. With a growl in my voice, I told them not to come any further, that this was a closed site and they had no business being here unless they were relatives of the previous occupant. My boss came out when he heard them and backed me up.

They were his aunties.

They lit a cigarette each after passing the packet around and even offered me one. I removed my gloves, unzipped my overalls, grabbed a drink, and went over to talk to them. They were very friendly despite our first encounter. They asked what we were doing and mentioned that it was bad inside the house.

I asked if they had been inside, and one of them answered, "We had to get some of her clothes," turning and facing the car as she spoke.

Sitting in the passenger side of the car smoking a cigarette was a young girl, no older than fifteen.

"This is his sister," they said. She glanced over at us and put her head back down, her hands consumed with a cigarette in one and her phone in the other.

"We'll be back tomorrow," said the aunt who did most of the talking. "We want to be here when her family arrives. We've never met them before." This wasn't going to be good, I thought to myself.

They roared off in their green Holden Commodore. We went back inside the house and were only there for about another half an hour when an older man arrived at the door, calling out to us. We greeted him at the front door wondering what other characters would grace us with their presence today. He had a professional attitude and tried to shake our hands, which were covered by blood-soaked gloves.

Unfortunately, he was only there to profit from the death of the young girl. He said he had heard about the murder on the two-way in his truck and only lived around the corner. As he thrust a business card into my hand, he said he had noticed that her car was still parked in the garden. Tow truck driver, you have to be kidding me. This was a housing commission area, and this low-life wanted to take away a car that was her only possession worth anything. He didn't shut up and kept fishing for information about what had happened, looking over our shoulders at the now clean hole in the wall. He rambled on about how he had seen a couple fighting across the road the night before, and when he heard that a young girl had been slain he knew where it was. He wasn't concerned about her in any way, he just wanted the car to profit from her death. When I had the opportunity to shut him up, I rudely said that we had a job to do and that he was interfering with a government operation, suggesting that he back off and never return. That did the trick and the low-life left, carless.

I sat outside near the skip to compose myself after all the craziness over the last hour, when I heard the rattling of a bike chain.

Two Aboriginal boys about ten years old pulled up on the footpath in front of me. They walked over, peered inside the skip and leant up against its rusty side.

"We want to see the dead girl," the more forward of the two boys announced.

My face screwed up as if I had been hit. They both started to move towards the front door and I jumped to my feet and stood in the doorway, legs and arms up against the wooden frame to block their view and entry inside.

"There's no one here," I told them.

"Let us look inside, please, please please!" the annoying boy yelled at the top of his lungs.

"Where are your parents?" I asked. "Do they know you're down here?"

They turned to each other and scattered.

"Don't come back here, boys!" I bellowed. "It's not a place for little boys." Nothing wrong with hurting an ego at an age when they were already pushing the boundaries. They rode off but then came back and waved to me, before disappearing for good.

My boss came outside and asked, "Who was that?"

"Just the neighbourhood kids," I said.

Surely, we wouldn't get any more visitors.

Back in the main bedroom, I began sorting through his belongings and found a disturbing letter written to his sister explaining that he was going down a bad path and no matter what happened to him, he wanted her to know he loved her. He said that if he wasn't around to give her the letter himself, whoever found it should pass it on to her. I put it in a box for his next of kin, already full of handwritten cards and letters addressed to him. I opened one of the letters and was saddened to discover that his own mother had been killed a few years before by her partner. If he really loved his sister, how could he leave her alone in this world? Motherless and now brother-less.

He would be sentenced in a few days for the crime he had committed and he wouldn't be running free for a long time. Out of sight and out of reach for the remainder of his youth.

The bad path he referred to in his letter was fuelled by the unprotected needles lying under his bed.

It took an entire day to mop up the mess and when the sun began going down, I wanted to get out of there. Even though the murderer was safely locked away, this was not a safe area. The thought that a girl just like me had been beaten to death in this house was horrible. The term 'beaten to a pulp' had taken on new meaning for me.

We had to go back the next day to make sure we had removed all signs of a struggle before the two families arrived. The girl's family didn't need to know what their daughter had gone through. She was resting now; the pain she had endured was over.

We arrived in plenty of time to inspect the property thoroughly and when I heard a knock at the door, I said to my boss, "They're here," thinking it was one of the families.

A Caucasian man stood alone leaning up against the doorframe, which until yesterday had been marked with a bloody handprint. He asked for the killer. You have to be joking, I thought.

"I don't know how to tell you this, mate, but you won't be seeing him for about twenty-five years."

"Oh yeah, I heard what he did," he mumbled. "I'm here because he said I could buy the fish tank for a hundred dollars."

"A hundred bucks?" I said. The tank was worth a hundred times more than that. It was so large it took up half of the lounge room wall and was at least one metre deep. "Go away!" I said. "How dare you! A girl just got killed by your mate and you're more concerned about scoring the most valuable item in here? Fuck … off."

Moments later I heard a car pull up and park on the grass out the front. The killer's family. My boss stopped what he was doing and went out to speak to them, letting them know that we did not want any confrontation here, least of all while we were inside the property. They felt the same way we did and were even a step ahead, having notified the police of what was about to possibly go down. We were all worried. These families had never met before and were about to come face to face in a situation where the nephew of one family had brutally bludgeoned to death the beautiful little girl of the other. I couldn't imagine how they must feel.

The police arrived shortly after, and the aunties came through the clean house and sorted through the sister's remaining clothing. She also came inside briefly. I smiled at her. I didn't know what else to do. They decided to take what they could for now, in time to get out before the deceased girl's family turned up.

When they finally did arrive, I was in the bathroom removing the last of the dried blood from the grout between the tiles in the shower. I'm certain that the police had made him have a shower before they took him away.

The family didn't say much as they walked from room to room, finally halting at the main bedroom where most of her belongings were. I did hear a slight sobbing when they noticed the gaping hole in the wall along the skirting board. They also realised that it had been made by her head. They wanted nothing of hers, no clothes, shoes or personal belongings. Just the car. They were arguing about the rego being out of date and that because the police were there, they couldn't drive it away. They never wanted to come back to this house. As soon as the police left, so did they, with the car and without crossing paths with the killer's family.

As the sun began its descent and silence fell, it was all over. The house looked like a refurbished property ready for new carpets. Once the walls were patched up, no one would ever know. Nevertheless, this wouldn't happen, because the house was in a housing commission estate in an area surrounded by the Aboriginal community, and it was now a forbidden place due to their customs and beliefs about death at the hands of another. The house would be left to stand empty for many years to come, until the memories faded and families moved on.

If you rent a property, you are never told the tales and secrets of its walls. It is only if you buy the house that the owners are bound by law to tell you. It's a way to buy a house cheaply – if you can live with the fact that blood was spilt.

As we left, I looked back down the hallway and thought about how this girl had slowly and painfully moved her way down to the comfort of the room they once shared. She was close to the front door when she received the first blow to her head, yet so far when the final evil act occurred.

I think of her regularly. I can never forget her face smiling down from the photos on the fridge. I wish I could forget his face.

Several times later, I drove past and noticed that the sheets had been replaced by curtains, which were always closed, and the lights were never on. The highway was eventually diverted and so I never drove past again.

I'll never know what happened to make love turn to hate.

Neighbourhood Watch

It was midsummer, the breeze had subsided and the heat was intense.

We were back in Brisbane at a death job. All we knew was that a man in his fifties had passed away and no one had seen him for at least a week. He must have been dead and rotting away alone for that time.

It was like a scene out of 'Desperate Housewives'. A neighbour was standing on her porch drinking her tea and staring down at us while we did our job.

It was a run-down, wooden, suburban home. A four-wheel drive was parked on the dried grass and it looked more valuable than the house.

It took the tea-drinking neighbour less than two minutes to start asking questions.

"Who are you? What are you doing?" she yelled between slurps. We politely answered her, not with what she wanted to know, just what she needed to know. We weren't intruders, we told her, we just had a job to do.

With my camera charged and ready to take photos and inspect the site, I walked up the rickety wooden stairs to the front door, being careful not to fall through. I noticed shards of glass on the top step. A colourful glass window in the front door had been smashed. A piece of wood had been nailed across the door to block entry. The police investigating the death had already told us we had to remove the wood, as the keys had been with the body at the time of death and had been taken as evidence.

The door swung open. Pieces of glass trapped in the door curtain behind fell onto the mustard-coloured carpet inside. Light danced off the shards of glass, and dust particles swirled in the light, floating in the air that stank so badly. I instantly turned around and smeared more Vicks under my nose. The smell was of damp surroundings mixed with the stench of death. When people pass away, they all smell slightly different. Time and diet are major factors in the odour released during decomposition, and this guy had been on a liquid diet. Cartons of Queensland 'XXXX' beer lined the walls.

Making my way back up the stairs, I saw that the deceased had been a hoarder. The place was cluttered with all sorts of belongings. The décor was more in keeping with what my great-grandmother would have loved, rather than a middle-aged man. Ornaments of all shapes, sizes and materials filled to overflowing the mismatched dusty glass cabinets. Beside an old grandfather clock, that looked to be the most valuable piece in the house, a large fridge stood against the wall, and a bar fridge took up a prominent position in the centre of the lounge room next to a shabby sofa.

Moving through the house, we entered the kitchen, which smelt of rotten meat oozing out of the two fridges whose power had been turned off days before. Fat from the stove was splattered up the walls and it had been painted over. I felt a lump in my throat and wanted to vomit. I didn't want to see any more and we hadn't even entered the room where his decomposing body had lain.

His bedroom was the last of three at the end of the house. The door had been left open so the smell was not contained, but it had seeped into the rest of the house, blending with the smell of mould and mothballs. An unmade bed was against the back wall. His blood and bodily fluids had been absorbed into the bed sheets and mattress. A dark patch on the wall surrounded by mould indicated that his head had been touching the wall when he died. His body would have expanded from the gases inside and blown him up like a balloon, pushing his skin and hair into the Gyprock.

When decomposition starts and the moisture is transferred onto another surface, mould begins to grow. When one life ends, another life form begins.

Once I got over the need to vomit, my feelings changed.

He had lived a sad life and I felt sorry him. Unlike other cases I'd attended, the circumstances surrounding his death weren't horrific. He had been suffering for years. I filled a large garbage bag with his medication. He'd had liver and kidney failure, as well as cancer throughout his body and a growth on his side the size of a basketball. No wonder he drank, and never cleaned his house. He probably hadn't done so in the five years since his parents had passed away. This explained the décor.

The neighbour was forever on her veranda looking over at the house as the hours turned into days. She told us that when he got drunk, he would throw defrosting meat onto her lawn, so they erected a fence. She said it should have been higher! She was a more annoying pest than the cockroaches that had nested in the grandfather clock.

The bedroom where the man had died was our first priority. The body fluids in that room had contaminated the rest of the house. I stripped the bed bare and the putrid stench of blood mixed with mould was gag-worthy. Here I was leaning over a bloody mattress, praying that my younger years as a gymnast would keep me balanced. I did not want to face-plant this mattress. We removed the mattress from the room and began cleaning the mouldy head stain from the wall. Then we took all the furniture out and began decontaminating the rest of the room. The sick man's blood had soaked into the floorboards next to the bed. The blood was old, and so all the blood-borne pathogens would have dissipated, but for resale, we used an antibacterial paint to repaint the floor. This was new for me, and I actually enjoyed doing it. The bright white paint and the smell of the paint made the dark and gloomy room fresh.

The rest of the rooms contained piles of worthless belongings, some obviously his mother's, untouched for many years, covered in cockroach and rat droppings, the latter green from rat bait. As I was boxing up valuable possessions, emptying the house, and getting rid of the stench oozing from every porous item, including the mustard carpet that needed to be ripped up, I made sure my mask was pulled tight against my face and my breath was very shallow. I was concerned for my health. I wondered how his relatives could have let him live in such filth with his poor health.

After a few days, shivers ran up my spine every time I entered the front door.

The nosy neighbour came in handy. She told us that one of his two sisters had arrived the day before we began cleaning to try to take possession of his belongings. Luckily, whoever was there that day didn't let her in, as she was not included in the will. She had sued her brother years before for fifty thousand dollars when their parents had died and left her nothing. He had then cut her out of his life and his will, leaving everything to his other sister who was coming the next day from Tasmania to go through his belongings and advise what we could dispose of and what was to be kept.

When the sister from Tasmania arrived, two women got out of the car. The other woman was the sister who had sued her brother and been cut out of his will, the brother whose remains we were mopping up. She was very well dressed and obviously had a lot of money, and the sad truth was she only lived around the corner.

They needed to be suited up, and I made sure I gave the cold-hearted sister the largest suit I could find. I watched carefully as they sorted through the family memorabilia, making sure they weren't taking any paperwork needed by the solicitor. I saw something: the sister who had no reason to be there put a dollar coin from his belongings in her pocket.

"Put that back," I said. "That's stealing, and I'll write it up in my report."

She was taken aback. "It's only a dollar!" she said.

"It's not yours," I retaliated, taking it out of her hand and placing it in her sister's. "This house and everything in it is yours," I said to the sister who was the beneficiary. "If you decide to give your sister a share in it, that's up to you. But if she touches anything else, you'll both have to leave!"

Walking into the spare bedroom, they said that nothing in there was their brother's. Someone else had lived here. Who was it and where were they? I wondered. I knew the neighbour would be able to tell me.

My boss and I went outside with them to the back of the house where two rusty old sheds stood side by side. There was so much stuff piled into the sheds I couldn't see past the rusty shovels and picks. Among the junk was a lot of rope, and tools on the shelves.

"He used to work for Telstra," I heard the sisters telling my boss.

The scrounge sister opened her greedy little mouth and said, pointing at the rope, "I want that. It will be no good to you. My husband can use that. Worth a whole ten dollars." I should have given it to her. There was a rat's nest inside. I would have loved to see the look on her face. But I stuck to my word: this woman was getting nothing if I had anything to do with it. It would hurt her more to leave empty-handed. Most of the items in the sheds were very old and rusty, and one of the sheds housed the belongings of the unknown flatmate. We were to tidy them up and make sure we got rid of all the rats. I was no longer shocked by the mummified carcass of a rat.

Cleaning the house took an entire week. Surprisingly, the bedroom where he had died and where his bodily fluids had leaked everywhere, and the mould-covered ornaments and dusty carpets that I breathed in with every breath, were not the worst things we had to deal with. The kitchen was the worst. The fridges were full of rotting food, the sink was full of plates with rotting food, and the kitchen benches either side of the sink needed to be removed.

My favourite part. Demolition.

The smell of rats grew stronger with each swing of the heavy sledgehammer. We were uncovering nothing short of a rat tomb. Deep under the cupboards were rats' nests full of dead rats buried in homes that had turned into their graves.

Elbow grease was needed to remove the grease splattered all over the walls.

When we finally finished, I would still never have eaten a meal at the dining room table.

The flatmate who resided in the spare bedroom was still a mystery. We had seen no sign of him. His clothing was old, as was the furniture. Everything was covered in an inch of dust. Through the dust, we could see that the furniture was a pale pink colour. An old wire-frame single bed was pushed up against one window, which had once had white lace curtains hanging there but were now stained a shade of yellow. I began packing up the flatmate's belongings, saving what was not contaminated by the smell that had oozed through the house from the decomposing body. Emptying the freestanding wardrobe, I found an extensive porn collection dating back to the seventies on the bottom shelf.

During a rest break, I noticed the lady next door pretending to water her plants and looking over her shoulder. "Does someone else live here?" I called out.

She told me that it was his best friend. A pleasant man, in his seventies, who worked in the mines. She told me she didn't think he knew about the tragedy. I asked if she had his phone number and she did. I was going to have to make the dreaded phone call. I needed to know what belonged to him and when he was going to be home. But first I needed to know if he knew what had happened. The phone began to ring and a kind voice answered. I told him my name, leaving out that I was a crime scene cleaner. I would tell him that later in the conversation. I told him that I was at the house and his friend had passed away. I can't remember if I waited for his response or not. It was a very hard thing to say. All I remember was that he was a little quieter than before. He said that he wouldn't be home for another week and I told him that I would wash and bag up all his belongings and put them in his bedroom and inform the sister to leave them alone, and if he needed anything, he could call me at any time.

I felt pain in my heart for this man. It's sad when someone leaves this earth, but the ones left behind are the most affected. We are the ones that go on living, remembering.

When the house was clean and almost empty, the beneficiary sister came back to go through the items that we had now put in the lounge room. Her other sister did not come. She told us that she had told her to back off. That she was greedy and seething from the fact that she had been left out of his will. She told us the reason, which we already knew. Tears flowed as she looked at old photos, followed by laughter when she sat on his old esky with wheels and fell onto her back on the floor. The things she did not want, she wanted us to give to his flatmate. She left them in the spare bedroom. He would want his mate to have these. It made me smile and I told her I would ring him to let him know. I wasn't dreading that phone call. When she left, she took the four-wheel drive, thanked us and drove away.

I looked forward to also pulling out of this driveway one last time.

Dusk was coming and in the soft light, the house was unrecognisable. A sense of achievement spread through me. It's a satisfying feeling knowing that the end is near. The floors were bare and the walls clean. Signs of life and death no more. Ready to be put up on the real estate merry-go-round. I closed the door behind me and nailed the wood back across.

From the outside, the house looked the same as when we had arrived. On the inside were a transformation and a tragedy that wouldn't be told, unless the neighbour was standing on her porch.

A Buddhist, a Muslim
and a Baby

A father's day card written by the deceased lay strewn on the floor. 'We love you Daddy, thank you for being the best Dad in the world,' it read.

The owners of the unit met us out the front. The wife was clearly shaken and she wouldn't step foot on the driveway. She greeted us and then sat back in the car. Her eyes told of the horror that had happened inside; they were wide, bloodshot and puffy. She had shed tears for the blood that had been shed. Her husband, an Englishman with sadness in his voice, said that his wife would never be returning to the home. She was haunted by the realisation that she had been in the unit next door unaware of the horror happening on the other side of the wall.

"She was like a daughter to us, and now she is gone. If only…" I heard him say under his breath.

We walked with him up the broken concrete steps leading to a porch with shrubs around the perimeter. A glass sliding door was closed, and the venetian blinds silently blocked the view of the destruction that lay behind. The owner unlocked the door for us and took a large step backwards.

"I'm going to leave you to it, I don't want to see inside!" he said. "Call me when you are done, I don't mind if it takes a few days. I can't face the horror. I wish I could forget. I'm never going to forget or forgive!" he continued.

I sat in an old off-white plastic garden chair and suited up, pulling my boot covers up over my shoes. Camera in hand, I took my last clean steps towards the door, pulled it open and pushed the blinds out of the way. The door opened up into a kitchenette. A TV stood in the opposite corner on a pale wooden TV cabinet. Mouldy food was on the table next to it, and the last feast was rotting in the sink. The shiny white tiles were marked with a trail of bloody footprints leading down to the back of the house. The now familiar blue of the amido acid had been used as in the other murder scene, and blue footprints throughout accompanied the bloody footprints. The polished tiles were slippery with blood and my boot covers made it worse. I managed to stay on my feet as though ice-skating. Treading carefully to dodge the footprints, we followed the trail down towards the bedrooms at the back of the unit. Another beautiful girl, killed at the hands of her lover. So close to the front door. A few metres away from friends and neighbours, yet she died alone in horror and pain on her bedroom floor. It's a haunting reality. The sanctum of a bedroom is usually filled with passion and happiness. Life had become a bloody mess of anger and hatred. Walking past the floral printed couch, we saw baby blankets and toys piled on top. Where's the baby? was my instant thought. That thought escaped my mind as soon as I entered the main bedroom. Blood covered the wall behind the bed. The dark blue bedspread was darkened by blood. A pungent sweet smell filled the air. I looked around to see where it was coming from. With the amount of blood in this room, I should have been engulfed in the sickening smell of it. But I wasn't. Down on the floor, heaped amongst clothing and a broken white wardrobe door was a large pile of white powder. Washing powder. It was a refreshing smell that took the edge off the smell of blood. At that moment I didn't realise it would have the most effect on me. The horror buried inside made finding skull fragments at the other murder scene pale in comparison.

We had finished looking around and made our way back to the front sliding door. Whenever we arrived at a job, we first had to ensure we had a safe work environment.

The owners had told us they didn't want to keep a single item. Nothing that would bring back memories of the pain and suffering that this murder had caused them.

He was from Thailand, a Buddhist; she was from Kazakhstan and a dedicated Muslim. Her family was flying over in the next few days. They didn't care about his family. We found nothing belonging to him in the unit except a credit card and schoolbooks with his name on them. That was it. He had packed up and cleared out.

A blood splatter led up from the bed onto the wooden headboard and the wall above. It showed that a sharp object such as a knife had been used and every time he had stabbed her, he had then pulled it back with such force that the blood from the blade had flicked off the edge and splattered drops in almost perfect lines on the once white wall.

I made my way around the bed frame and the mattress. The mattress was so drenched with blood that most of the padding inside had to be removed before we could put the mattress into the skip bin. With a small spade, I began shovelling the pile of white washing powder that was heaped onto the ground at the foot of the bed into a hazardous materials bag. Something about the powder didn't look right. It was tinged pink and got darker in colour the closer I got to the carpet. I presumed that blood had soaked into the powder until I touched something that had a different texture. It was soft but harder than the fluffy powder. I picked up a lump and looked at it closely. I instantly felt sick and cried out. It was part of her stomach. He had slashed her so badly that her insides had opened up and fallen out onto the floor.

It made sense now. He had stayed in that house for an estimated nine hours after killing her, the police had told the owners, carefully packing up his belongings while his wife lay butchered on the bedroom floor and his baby sat on the couch in the lounge room, unaware of what Daddy had just done to Mummy. The smell of the blood and internals intensifies as time goes on, as they are now outside her body. The sweet smell of washing powder acted like a deodoriser for him. Masking the smell that churns in the pit of your stomach.

He had trudged blood throughout the house. There were bloody clothes on the bathroom floor, although the ones he had worn during the heinous crime had been washed and were still in the washing machine. The washing machine had a bloody handprint on the lid. He had showered, gone to the toilet and left only the spare room with her clothes in it untouched. A suitcase half packed, or half unpacked, was on the floor. If she had been planning to go away or had been away, no one would ever know. She is now in a peaceful place where no one can hurt her anymore. We threw all her clothing out. It seems wrong to dispose of clothing that are in good condition, although I'm sure no one shopping at an op shop wants a dead girl's clothing on their back.

We ripped up all the carpets and the underlay, took off the wardrobe doors, and left the house gutted. The only structure that remained was the walls, which would be repainted in a different colour. The same colour can trigger the memory of anyone who witnesses a crime scene. A couch can be replaced in a different style, yet if it is the same colour, the memory is triggered. Replace it with the same style but a different colour, and it has no effect. The mind is powerful, although it is tricked easily.

The crime, murderer and aftermath was found out when a lady at the local church he attended was concerned with his erratic behaviour and requests. He took the baby there and told her that he was due to go to Thailand that afternoon and his wife had run away, leaving him with nowhere to turn. He couldn't take the baby to Thailand and asked if she could look after his child for a few days until he returned. She took the child but called the police straight away. She was fearful for the child's life and the safety of the wife. She had every right to be. Mum hadn't run away, she had run as far as she could and been brutally stabbed almost forty times trying to escape him.

He was tracked down at the airport and arrested after the police dashed to his last known residence and saw what we saw, minus the body. I don't normally wish ill thoughts on anyone, but I hope he rots in his cell.

I had an intense feeling of sadness the whole time I was in the house. I'm glad he took all his photos. His is one face I don't want to remember.

I still wonder what became of the child. Who would be the one to tell the tale of what Daddy did to Mummy? The murderer is not the only one to live with what he did for the rest of his life. His own child will live with it for the rest of his. Weddings, graduations, life's journeys, he will go them all alone.

Liquid Diet

I was called to a job south of the border between Queensland and New South Wales. They couldn't tell me much but they knew that the place stank. The man had only been dead for a few hours, so that would mean one thing: faeces, poo, shit. Whatever you want to call it, it's my least favourite thing to clean and decontaminate. People turn their noses up at a baby's nappy, so just imagine a grown man who has shit his pants and all over the floor.

It took me two and a half hours to get there. I sang merrily along to the radio, trying not to think of what lay kilometres ahead.

I pulled up to the pet-friendly caravan park, noticing the word 'pet' instantly. I was soon to realise that caravan parks weren't just for people holidaying with their families. It was a society for the elderly to live out their last days on earth.

I met with the owner on a gravel driveway. He was in his early forties and a fit-looking man with long dark wavy hair pulled loosely into a ponytail. Like everyone else, he looked shocked as I climbed out of the car.

"Will you need help?" he asked me with a raised eyebrow.

"No thank you, I'm perfectly capable," I responded.

He gave me a brief run-through of what had happened.

The old saying 'liquid diet' was something I used to associate with people on diets. I was again about to experience what it meant, in this line of work.

The man had died in his caravan with his cat by his side. The police were still waiting on the coroner's report to determine the cause of death. Perhaps his body had just had enough and shut down.

The longer a body is left unattended, the more fluids it releases. First, waste, then fatty fluids along with some blood. After that, the decomposition sets in. Skin, hair, it all comes off the bone. Like a well-cooked lamb shank. As he had only been there for a few hours and rigor mortis was just setting in, only the first had happened.

Arriving at the front of the caravan, which had an annex attached to the side, I unpacked and set myself up for the task ahead.

The manager left me, saying he would be back to help. He wanted to keep the costs down as he would be the one out of pocket due to this unfortunate event. However, I think he believed I wasn't capable of doing it on my own.

Through the murky glass sliding doors I could see inside the annex attached to the caravan, where most of his belongings were. Pushing my face closer to the glass, I could see the place was stained throughout. I had been told by the caravan park owner he lived alone, apart from the companionship of his pet cat. The tenants from other caravans had helped clean up most of the cat faeces that was inside, so I only had to deal with the smell, human waste and to disinfect the premises. It would have taken a lot for those people to come into the space and do what they did, willingly helping others regardless of the situation, with no reward.

The caravan was small. It had a kitchen sink with basic utensils piled up against one wall. A built-in lounge faced a table on the opposite wall and a bunk bed was nailed into the back wall.

I was more than prepared for what I could be facing and had my gas mask pulled tight across my face.

Brown liquid was smeared across the lino. This was what I had been called in to clean. As I tackled the worst first, wiping up the faeces by hand and gagging into my gas mask, I heard a knock on the sliding door.

An old frail looking lady was standing in the doorway. I stopped what I was doing and went to greet her.

"How much to clean my kitchen, love?" she asked in a husky voice.

I frowned. Was she trying to be a comedian? I looked at her, puzzled, and she continued.

"Such a shame, wasn't it, I told him he drank too much." She went on. "I really hate cleaning my kitchen, I'm just getting too old. How much would you charge me, lovey?" Trying my hardest to remain professional, I responded with, "I'm sorry, but for what I charge you would be better off getting a new kitchen. You need a regular house cleaner. I only do it if someone has died. Do you have a dead body in your kitchen?" I just couldn't help myself. I shouldn't have. I didn't know if she was going to burst into tears. In the moment it took me to blink, she was gone.

Before I re-suited, the manager of the caravan park pulled up in his truck. The roads around the caravan park were too tight to bring a skip through so we had decided to put the furniture into the back of his Ute. He wanted to strip down the caravan and start again, as if washing the walls down and removing the furniture would remove the memories. The number on the side of the caravan would always be a reminder of what had happened inside. Only in time would this man's death become an urban tale.

The lino needed to come up as it was cracked and marked with human faeces. Stanley knife in hand, I carefully began cutting along the flooring. Double-gloved and taped to my suit, I peeled back the section where I had cut.

Gravy is the best description I have to describe what I saw. A thick, brown liquid was embedded in the cracks and had spread underneath. The smell was overwhelming. I would have known this if I hadn't been wearing a full face gas mask. As for my trusty side-kick in his dust mask, a muffled sound escaped from his mouth. It was a cross between the word 'fuck' and a womanly scream. Then he said, "I can't do this. Call me when you're done," and he was out of there. I had been distracted and forgot that I was waving around the tarnished lino in my hand.

Turning back around, I thought, how the hell am I going to get this sharp-edged shit-covered filthy material into a garbage bag? As I rolled it up, it flicked open, spitting faeces all over my arm. I was going to be sick.

Blood on my overalls I can handle, but not faeces. The next ten minutes were a blur. Faeces were all over the outside of the garbage bags and so I had to double-bag everything. Once the lino was up, the bare floor was not a refreshing sight. It was like a folded children's painting imprinted on both sides. Take two, here we go again. Bending down with one hand on my knees, I wiped up a grown man's faeces until there was nothing left. Still wearing my gas mask, I don't think I took a breath through the entire process. As soon as I'd cleaned it, I jumped up, stripped off my protective clothing, and ran out of the caravan to lather myself with hand sanitiser.

Composing myself, I re-entered the caravan and began to disinfect and remove the smell of the owner, in readiness for the next.

By the time I was ready to remove all the belongings, the local tip was closed for the day, and so I wiped them all down, sanitising them as I went, and put them around the side of the caravan out of sight.

The most memorable and exhilarating part of this day was sliding a hose through an open window once I had sprayed the walls, ceiling and floor with an enzyme solution and disinfectant, and blasting the walls full bore.

Caravans are built with materials that are used in most outdoor sheds, so nothing was going to be destroyed by the cleansing water. Once I had finished, I turned the hose onto myself, cleansing both my body and my mind.

The manager of the caravan park was very happy with my clean. I didn't need it, but I had earnt his respect. He hadn't been able to do what I did. I wanted to be the best, so I'd learnt from the best. Now I am one of the best.

Whenever I drive past the caravan park on my way to see friends down the coast, I look at the sign with the dog on it. 'Pet friendly', it reads. Inviting! Especially to those who want a family get away.

Rubbish Tomb

"I'm going to take you to the premises so you can see what you're in for tomorrow," my boss told me.

This has to be bad, I thought.

Looking at the house it was close to a hundred years old and the spider webs hanging from the windows gave it an eerie, haunted feel. We walked around to the back door, where multiple gas masks lay on the grass.

"You're going to need this," my boss said, handing me a mask and VapoRub to put under my nose. He opened the back door, but only a metre or so wide. It looked as if he couldn't open it any further. "Go in and check it out for yourself," he told me, warning me to be careful where I stepped.

I could smell methane gas even through my mask, as the bacteria was multiplying in the decomposition of the waste, infecting the air with the stench of rotten eggs. Although that was nothing compared to what I was about to face.

Rubbish, rubbish, rubbish, a metre high in most places. A piece of corrugated iron sat on top of the rubbish leading to the back door. I carefully made my way as far in as I could. I have never seen so many VB bottles in my life. Later in the job we had to call the council to bring us twenty recycling bins. The man driving the recycling truck was as shocked as we were. He said he didn't pick up anywhere near as many from all the pubs and nightclubs on a Saturday night.

I could only see into the kitchen and down into the hallway. How do you even start to remove any of this? Where do you begin? I was exhausted from just looking at the task ahead. The house and contents were worth peanuts. If he hadn't told his daughter before he had passed that he had hidden money in there, a bulldozer would have been a great way to clean this place up. We weren't there to be crime scene cleaners, we were to be cleaners and treasure hunters.

Closing the door behind me, I was at least now better prepared for what I was in for over the next few days. We went back to our motel, had dinner and went to bed.

I had nightmares that night. Spiders crawling over my bare skin, and being buried alive in rubbish. I thought I was ok. My subconscious was not.

What I saw over the next week and a half cannot be easily described. The house stood on a large block of land and was situated at the back of the property, shadowed by an old willow tree. Driving by, it looked like any other house on the street. The lawns were unkempt but that was nothing unusual.

People who rough it out on the streets live better than this man did.

I started the next morning. Opening the back door as far as I could, I had the same feeling as the day before, a drop in the pit of my stomach.

I was unsteady on my feet. How did an eighty-year-old man walk around on top of this, let alone sleep on top of it? We had been told he had died of a heart attack in his bed. He had been there for a week, but no one had been concerned about him. The neighbour next door was the first to raise the alarm. She was a sweet lady who I couldn't thank enough. She let me use her bathroom whenever I needed. Such a simple requirement that in this house was impossible. We couldn't get into the house far enough to see what state the toilet was in. I could only imagine, or I didn't want to. The rubbish was dense, a mixture of bottles and rotting food and cartons, so thick that the rubbish on top was compacting into the rubbish below, turning it into mush and liquefying. The carpets were soaked through with a liquid that was so gross, even with double gloves on I didn't want to touch it.

Because a bulldozer was out of the question, my only other option was a shovel and a rusty old bin to begin sifting through the tip. When the bottom of the bin fell out, we went through about five hundred garbage bags for the job. The photos speak louder than a thousand words, but I can't show you the photos.

In the house of a hoarder, the contents are usually piled up in the room they belong in. A shower full of soap, a toilet cupboard full of toilet rolls. This house was like the local dump. There was no formality. He drank tea and smoked cigarettes sitting on the toilet, and filled the bathtub with tea bags and discarded milk cartons. He couldn't use the toilet for its actual purpose anymore. It was full of faeces and urine that had clogged all the piping and was oozing over the edges with the seat pushed down on top. His toilet was a yellow bucket in the corner, slopping around with human waste. Flies and maggots were churning around inside. It wasn't the only one. In the bedroom where he had died, a blue bucket similar to the one in the bathroom was placed in the right-hand corner on top of a mountain of rubbish. It should have registered after my encounter with the yellow bucket. I reached for it and it toppled over. Brown liquid poured out and like mountain lava spewing down from a mountain of rubbish, it headed straight for me. The smell was so bad my boss ran outside like a bull through a gate. I had just made my job so much harder. The rubbish at the bedroom door was now wet with sloppy shit.

His bedroom and final resting place had the most amount of junk in it. The mattress had been stuffed with plastic bags to fill up the holes inside it.

We were later to find out that the room had once been his son's. They'd had a strained relationship. In some psychotic way, it explained why he would destroy the room to such a degree. It took me a whole day of shovelling to get into that room and make a visible dent in the debris. Inside the bedside table, that we couldn't see until we dug it out from underneath a mountain of newspapers and soft drink bottles, we found his only valuables. Two gold and ruby rings, with an initial on each. They would be called vintage. To me they looked like a pirate's treasure.

His only living relative was his daughter, a fat, frumpy, money-grabbing woman. Sometime before his death, he had told her he had money saved and stashed. So, days before we got there, the, greedy, disgrace of a human that she was had been digging up the ground inside a self-built garden shed that he had slept in at times, on a mouldy, yellow, stained, single, foam mattress. She had carelessly filled the holes back in, in an attempt to cover her tracks. She couldn't get into the house to search for his life savings so she thought there might be buried treasure in the garden. I had thought that only drug dealers and people living in the forties did that. Her father had died inside a home that she had not stepped foot inside for twenty years, the neighbour told us.

People grieve in different ways.

You don't have to shed a tear to show you are hurting inside, but digging up around a soiled mattress that your own flesh and blood has slept on to find his buried treasure isn't the way most of us would mourn a loss so fresh. When her quest for the treasure came up empty, she told us that his life savings weren't in the bank so they must be in the house. He had told her so. She had us looking inside thin curtain rods, inside the ripped mattresses he was found dead on, and inside the washing machine – the cleanest place in the house. If only she had cared more about her father and less about the money, maybe things wouldn't have ended the way they had. He might have been happier and not become an alcoholic. She might have ended up with a penny or two. Lonely men do lonely things. Alcohol becomes their reason to live, their best friend and in the end, their worst enemy.

We were soon to discover that he had been a very sick man. Mixed in with the beer bottles were bottles that had been opened, emptied, filled up again and resealed. He had been recycling and using the bottles as a toilet, carefully sealing the contents of his urine with the lid, after each beer he consumed. The bottles from down in the depths of the rubbish contained a yellow liquid; the ones placed on top were the colour of red wine. He had been dying slowly. Blood was mixed in with his urine. I lined them up on the washing machine and had the unpleasant task of emptying them one by one. I can no longer look at 'Tooheys New' the same way. He was shitting in buckets and pissing in bottles. He was dying a slow and painful death alone, surrounded only by waste, spiders and rats.

The lovely lady next door would stick her head over the fence when we took a break outside to play with the blue-tongue lizards hiding in the grass. She told us about his life, and about the daughter. His wife had passed away some twenty years earlier. Like most women born in the early 1900s, she had done everything for him, so when she passed he was lost. He trashed every room in that house. Every room except for hers. Her rat-chewed clothing still hung inside the wooden, dated, freestanding wardrobe. Her shoes, handbags and pearls covered in dust were inside plastic bags at the bottom of the wardrobe. Untouched and undisturbed in twenty years, they were the pieces of a puzzle to a broken heart.

We moved through the house like moles tunnelling underground, slowly making progress. It was a never-ending story of booze, food, and dead rats, spiders and cockroaches. A dog kennel was out the back, but the dog had passed away years earlier. Lucky thing! Death is a better place than living in this filth. Even for an animal.

It took a whole week to remove the rubbish and to be left with the empty shell of the house. The daughter wanted to save as much of the furniture as she could, although unfortunately, most of it had been destroyed by the rotting garbage surrounding it. She even wanted to save the bathtub, stained black on the inside with mould. She wanted it as a drinking tub for her horses. I felt like smashing it with my sledgehammer just so those poor horses didn't have to drink the water that would become contaminated from the tub. There was one item of furniture that looked like it was worth about fifty dollars, and she was adamant that we save it, later to find out that she only wanted to sell it.

The house and contents weren't worth much, but she hadn't yet realised that the land it stood on, situated near a river and on a double block, was worth close to half a million dollars. She should have knocked the house down and sold the land on its own, without spending a cent on cleaning up. If she hadn't searched for buried treasure, she would have saved money.

The house was almost inviting once it had been emptied. The only tell-tale sign that anything was out of the ordinary was that the floor in the kitchen needed replacing. The fridge had leaked and dripped onto the wooden floor over many years, rotting it right through to the core.

When we closed the door for the last time after two weeks, it was satisfying to see how far we had come. No more rats nesting in old garbage; no redback spiders hanging from the roof in webs that looked like cotton candy with dust particles, the red markings on their backs a warning to stay away. Cockroaches by the thousands were now gone, and all signs of the previous life had been washed away with the dirt from the walls.

I've driven past once since then. The house still stands empty behind the willow tree.

The Circus is in Town

Old MacDonald had a farm, but he let them roam in the house. At first, I couldn't help but laugh at the sixty-four cats, two dogs, donkey, horse, pony, many chickens, ferrets, and rabbits that had all been allowed to roam in one big house. The cows from the outside paddock were free to come into the house, creating more filth.

And let's not forget the hermaphrodite. More on that later.

I came onto the job a few weeks after the team had been there, because they needed extra help.

The stories I had heard and the photos I had seen were out of this world. The house was an amazing structure. Only someone in my field of work would be able to see past the fly faeces covering every inch of the house and the smell oozing from the walls and wooden floors.

The condition of the house was only discovered when the homeowners failed to pay their mortgage and the bank sent someone to change the locks. Only then did they realise what problems lay ahead. They had already had someone come in to take away all their belongings, to prevent the owners from coming back to the property, just as we had done on the Rockhampton job with the drug lab and the bikies. We were told that the man who had removed the items had had to burn his clothing afterwards because of the smell in the house. They were beyond washable. The putrid clothing would have made a farmer after he cleaned out a pig trough smell like roses.

The house was situated on a five-acre block. It had multiple bedrooms and lounge rooms and a kitchen fit for a king – or at least it had been once. The rooms at one end of the house were duplicated at the opposite end. This stunning house was clouded by filth, to the point where they had had to bring in a bulldozer to remove the soil from around its perimeter, so contaminated was it by hazardous waste, both animal and human. A shipping container was the only sign to the outside world that anything unusual was going on. They had emptied all the furniture out of the house and put it in there. The smell inside made my eyes water.

The empty house had all the windows and doors wide open to get fresh air wafting through. Flies swarming in a circular motion in the middle of every room were now the only life form left inside the house, besides us. I was shocked at the sights and smells as I walked through each room.

It was a cold, rainy day in a small town near Goulburn in country New South Wales. The town had only one bakery, a post office and a pub with the fire burning brightly. The pub was the only place I felt warm the whole time I was there, and I wish I could say I spent the time sitting around the fire drinking a beverage, but it was the only place I could visit the toilet. The bathrooms in the house had all been ripped up previously by one of the crime scene technicians. It was preferable that the plumbing pipes were the only sign of them left. On my frequent trips to the pub toilet, I got strange stares from the locals who were trying to work out who I was. We were the talk of the town, and the town *was* talking.

Animal cruelty and mental illness ran rampant behind the walls of that house. The kitchen was like something out of a hotel, with large benches and the biggest appliances I had ever seen. However, they had converted the kitchen into a chicken coop, with chicken wire along the benches. They had their own chicken farm, right there in the kitchen. No need to go out and get eggs from the back of the garden, I assumed. The kitchen had thick yellow fat all over one wall, blending in with the fly faeces. The Gyprock had to be removed to halfway up the walls, because they were swollen with cat urine. Cat urine smells so strongly of ammonia that unless it is cleaned up straight away, the smell is forever imbedded in the material.

One cat is bad enough; sixty-four is out of control. Stray cats had initially bred with their cat and the vicious cycle had continued. They'd enticed them by feeding all of them, and then had not been able to get rid of them. It took the RSPCA days to catch all of the cats, and some were so feral that they needed to set traps in order to catch them.

The kitchen was not the only place where the Gyprock had to be removed. It had to be taken out of almost every room in the house, uncovering the skeleton of the house frame to the brick on the other side. We also had to remove the wooden flooring. It is an exhilarating feeling having a chainsaw in hand and cutting through the floorboards down to the earth beneath. It was like a childhood dream, or it was, until I was washing the ceiling later in the day, not looking where I was going, and came crashing through the hole I'd made to the earth below, one leg still inside the house, the rest of me a metre below.

In the first lounge room, the smallest room of the house with French doors and elegant gold handles, a rusty chain lay on the floor with bolt cutters beside it. The panels on the doors were stained all over with an unusual substance, a murky yellowish mould-like growth. Opening the doors, we saw that all the walls but one had been removed. The remaining wall had the appearance of having been eaten by rats the size of horses. I was told that this was where they had kept their beloved dog, a German shepherd who had been locked up for ten years here, never allowed to walk on the grass or smell the fresh air. The story down at the local pub was that the animal had attacked the postman many years back, and instead of putting him down they had kept him chained up in this room. The poor animal had been so desperate and distraught that he tried eating through the walls. The marks on the windows were from his excretions. He had to be put down after being mistreated in this way, a sad ending to a sad life.

Halfway through this job, we received a call and a horrendous photo about a job in Alice Springs. A man had been evicted from his house and in spite, he had changed the locks and locked a horse inside the house, before casually walking away. It was weeks before anyone realised what he'd done. The horse was left with no water or food and the poor animal died on the floor and began decomposing. The photo showed no hair, only skin and bone, its insides out and a massive pool of blood and bodily fluids. There are some evil individuals in this world.

There were more surprises to come. Sleeping on its own mattress in the end bedroom was a pony. The bedroom was bigger than mine and had its own bathroom. A horse wasn't so lucky. It was in a small caravan, converted into a makeshift stable, parked at the rear of the house. Barely big enough to sleep one person, let alone a horse.

The place looked like a circus. In fact, it did come with a half-man, half-woman attraction. The woman of the house was a hermaphrodite.

The shed out the back, a barn-cum-workshop, looked as if a hurricane had swept through it. The metal sheeting was bent and twisted in all directions. Manure was piled metres high, mixed with hay. A donkey called this place home. He too had tried to escape, belting the metal-sheeted walls with his hind legs.

Although the house wouldn't be finished for weeks, my time had come to return home. I needed to be available in case another job came in closer to home, so I didn't see the finished result, just as I hadn't seen the starting point.

The only thing that had been missing from this place was the big top tent.

Home is Where the Heart Is

I got the phone call for the next job and was told to be there within an hour. I wasn't looking forward to what awaited me. The workers of an electrical company had described how a maintenance room in a council building had been a haven for junkies. There were piles of vomit and syringes everywhere, they said.

I drove though the busy streets of Brisbane and pulled into a side street that ran parallel to the river. It was beautiful, a sanctum of peace from the world surrounding it. Hundreds of scooters in a crooked row leaned up against a stone brick wall. A steel-framed ladder led up high onto a Pebblecrete platform with a solid metal door.

When I climbed up the ladder onto the platform, I opened the broken door expecting to find what I'd been told, vomit and syringes, but instead, there were just remains of crisps on the floor.

Walking through the damp concrete room, I found all the essentials that young girls would need: toiletries, pillows and clothing, a mirror, makeup. There were also handwritten notes crumpled up on the floor expressing how hard life was living on the streets. From the tone of the notes and the word of passers-by, the girls were no older than sixteen.

With people's busy lives, we don't take notice of what is going on around us, or even care. I was working on a main road, in full sight of hundreds of people, but few made eye contact with me and if they did, they soon looked down, as if I didn't exist. Much as they would have done to these girls who were living inside the maintenance room.

The job was quick and fast. I was in and out within the hour.

Weeks later, an email was forwarded to me. It was from the council worker who had stayed with me to unlock the broken door and make sure whoever had been living in the squat was no longer there. The council had wanted the job to be safe and quiet. You don't always get a lot of satisfaction or rewarding words in this job, as it's practically a secret industry, so to know that I was appreciated was a great feeling. He applauded me for my work and efforts, although he told me the homeless had broken in again through the door he had fixed and he was worried about what he might find in there again.

One week later, I was back at the same address overlooking the river. The room was the perfect place for someone who had nowhere to go. It had power, lighting and an amazing view of the Brisbane River. It was an annoyance for the government but it brought a smirk to my face knowing this would just keep happening. It's a sad reality that while many of us are tucked up comfortably on the couch watching TV, others have nothing more than a newspaper and a park bench. No matter what brought them to that path in their life, most are still worthy people.

This time, the room had been a dwelling for a group of men. Condoms, beer bottles and cards were scattered on the floor. A nasty surprise lay in wait in the dark corner ahead.

They had been using the dark depths of the corner as a toilet.

Again, I was in and out in a short time. The passers-by didn't even notice the suited-up girl above them. Businessmen, with only business on their mind. People walk by the homeless and don't even look at them. Why would they look at me?

The job wasn't the goriest, the most interesting, or the most rewarding. It was a reality into the underworld of the homeless and the less fortunate.

When I now walk past the homeless, even if I don't give them a dollar, I give them a smile. Kindness is a gift everyone can give, if they want to.

Never Judge a Book by its Cover

The suburb is known for its mansions and waterfront views, and its high society, churchgoing folk. But they didn't notice the mould-covered windows or the rats running in and out of the holes they had made through the walls.

She was well known in her community and regularly attended church. Behind her mansion walls, however, she suffered an illness that no one could see. She endured obsessive compulsive disorder, which caused her to hoard obsessively. Physically, she looked fine. Her hair was blow-dried every day. Little did her community know that she had to have it washed every week. She hadn't used her shower in years. How could she when it was full of toiletries and rats. The front door hadn't been opened in over twenty years.

It would take two men and me many backbreaking hours and hundreds of garbage bags to clean up.

Her situation could have continued until she left this earth if it hadn't been for a leaky toilet that created a waterfall from the upstairs into the lounge room below. No one would have ever known. She planned on leaving her house to the church in her will, and they were the first people she called upon for help. The pastor organised for someone to have a look. The tradesman somehow fixed the ceiling, without even using a ladder due to the mountains of rubbish. This chain of events led to helping her start her life afresh.

Every room told the story of how the disease in her mind controlled her existence. The house had been beautiful. It had two large lounge rooms downstairs, a dining room, kitchen, laundry, and bathroom. Upstairs was another lounge room, four bedrooms, another two bathrooms, and a long hallway. But each room unveiled something even grosser than the previous one.

The methane smell was so toxic it physically took my breath away, despite the filtered mask pulled tight over my nose and mouth.

I love all animals, big and small, and I am a sucker for a fur coat, faux of course. This lady had several of the real deal hanging in amongst the filth. They were exquisite, apart from the rat urine and droppings that weighed down the coats, which still had five-thousand-dollar price tags attached.

The kitchen was filled two metres high with food, expiry dates five years back. The food at the bottom of the piles had decomposed into a slushy brown mess. Cockroaches by the thousand were scurrying out of tins and burrowing back into the darkness. The dining rooms were cluttered with junk of all sorts, so high and unstable it amazed me how she could drift so effortlessly over the carnage without a single stumble. Even in my steel caps and in protective gear from head to toe, I had to be careful with my footing not to slip and fall into the chaos below. Rats had consumed every corner, leaving gaping holes. Wherever they could walk, they had chewed, including above light switches and along the dividers that separated the walls from the ceilings, chewing into the Gyprock. The smell of rat urine would have been overwhelming if it hadn't been for the rubbish that was soaking it up and blending it all into one.

The furniture was expensive and luxurious yet destroyed by rotting rubbish that lay around it. All the flooring was covered in metre depths of rubbish, placed purposely in each location. Each item she purchased to fill her home had a place and a reason to be there. Her shower was overflowing with toilet paper rolls. The bathroom cabinets had soap cakes melted together. The cupboards in the kitchen were packed solid with expired tins of food full of gases. These exploded at the slightest touch and they had made black ring marks on the shelves.

It was like walking on land mines, with stomach-churning surprises at each step.

The upstairs looked less contaminated at first glance, but how wrong we were. The worst was yet to come. The carpets were soaked from the sweating of compacted items that lay on its once pink surface. A lone armchair was surrounded by newspapers that dated back to the seventies. A rug lay over the chair, with the stains of body secretion from someone sitting on it with no pants on. I gagged in disgust. I still cringe.

The owner of the house was a very sweet lady. Unlike other similar jobs I'd encountered so far in my career, she was the first person I'd met who was still living. Once we had moved all salvageable items downstairs and decontaminated them, we called her carer to bring her over to assess the site. It broke my heart to see her being told to sit in a chair surrounded by her multitude of possessions and to pick only one of each.

How can anyone pick just one of each item from their belongings? Even with her clothing, the carer made the decision about what she could keep, without so much as looking at her first to see her reaction. Every time I found something new, I would pass it to her first to let her make up her own mind.

I myself struggle to get rid of clothing that I haven't worn in a while. I always think I might want to wear it again if it comes back into fashion. I give myself the one-year rule. If I haven't worn it in that time, out it goes. There is a little hoarder in each of us.

It was sad watching the tears stream down her cheeks as she was forced to make decisions she wasn't capable of or ready for.

My favourite part of this tale is that little did they know when they left her to her own devices in her one-bedroom rented apartment while we cleaned her home, she used to catch a taxi to the grocery store, stock up on food, leave it on the floor, and do it all again the next day. I smiled when I heard this, even though I realise it's not funny, it's sad. The only reason it made me smile was that the woman appointed to look after her was nothing short of a ball-breaker. She was a member of the church, and the church was the sole beneficiary of her will. They were trying to keep costs down, so there was more left over for their greedy pockets. The ball-breaker had already organised a garage sale and wanted to know where the most valuable items were. They had forgotten she was still alive and breathing. She didn't want to leave her home, and with the money she had in the bank she was able to afford a carer. The church didn't agree. Fortunately, they were overruled by her doctor and she was able stay in her home with a carer rather than be put in a home. She was fragile and the shock of a move could have killed her.

The elderly are easily forgotten, yet some of them have seen more in their lives than we could ever imagine. Their storytelling is a bore to most people, but I wish I had the time to sit and talk to her. Especially about her clothes.

She was nothing short of fabulous.

Triple Zero

I hadn't heard any news reports and so I guessed the reporters hadn't yet heard about it.

The police asked me to go straight there, no questions asked. It was already late afternoon, and all they told me was that a man had been in a gun fight with the police, it was a high-risk job, and I needed to be finished in two hours. The pressure was on. In the past, the time frames I had been given were days, not hours.

The police were still on site when I pulled up and the blue and white chequered tape was the only sign that something had happened at the property.

A police officer and a representative from the department of housing met me. A pop-up tent had been set up on the neighbour's lawn and two more police sat with their feet up on a fold-out picnic table reading the newspaper.

I introduced myself, continued past the men and walked through the rusted old iron gate and around the side of the house along the freshly mown grass. On the concrete flooring of the carport, I encountered what I had only ever seen in movies until then. It didn't look real. The outline of a man's body with a bloodstain near the head. It looked like something children had drawn with chalk. Arms by his side, legs straight out in front of him. It was something I had always feared seeing, and it made me sad.

I walked back out to the car to collect my thoughts, assess a strategy to clean and get my equipment.

As I walked back to the house, one of the police officers in the fold-out chairs commented, "I don't care what you do as long as you get rid of that body outline."

I was taken aback. "That's not the way I work," I responded. "The main reason I'm here is to remove any biohazard waste that could harm the family or anyone who lives in the area."

Again in a monotone, his response was short and sharp. "When his kid comes home she won't want to see where Daddy got shot. I don't care what it takes but get rid of it!"

I told him I would and that the family would not be allowed near the house until I had finished. The outline would be removed but when I was ready. As I walked away, I told him the site was closed. I wasn't to be disturbed and didn't want anyone with me due to the time constraint.

In the garden, medical waste lay strewn around near the body outline. He had still been alive when they took him away. I leaned over the outline to look at it, and visions flashed through my mind. Separate yourself from this scene, I told myself.

I collected water from the tap around the back. There were dump trucks and other children's toys where the children had played. This eerie place had once been full of life.

Would it return to being that way? Was the man still clinging to life in the hospital?

I wanted to know. I just didn't need to.

The grass leading to the edge of the concrete carport floor was covered in blood-soaked bandages that the ambulance officers had used on his head. Both the grass and the concrete were tarnished red from soil and blood. Three black crosses marked the spot where bullet casings had fallen in the place the police shooters had stood, although the casings had been removed. Some old outdoor furniture was splattered with blood, blending in with the mould that had grown from being left out in the elements. I began mopping up the blood and removing the chalked outline. I used paint thinner on the crosses, which were very close to the outline. I had to pull up grass and leave patches of dirt where the blood had seeped into the grass.

The clean-up was relatively quick and easy. The crosses were still slightly visible, although they were not a danger to anyone, and the concrete had to be painted. The blood was gone but it had left a stain that could not be removed. It isn't common for blood to stain a surface, but in some cases it happens and this was one of them. It is harmless, but it brings back memories. I had paint in my vehicle with an antibacterial agent that I could use, but I first had to ask the delegate from the Department of Housing.

I packed up my belongings and filled out the paperwork. The sun was now going down. One plain-clothes police officer was still waiting under the pop-up tent reading the paper, and the man from the Department of Housing was waiting in his car.

I walked over to it and asked him, "Would you like to inspect the site? There's something I'd like to show you."

We walked back down to the carport and he looked around. I showed him the faded black crosses.

"It looks perfect, thank you," he said. "We'll repaint the carport ourselves, but thank you for asking. The house hasn't been cared for too well so there's a lot of work to be done inside and out."

We walked back to his car and he shook my hand before leaving.

The police officer rose from his chair and walked over to me. "All finished?" he asked, stating the obvious. "I'll just take one look and then I'll be on my way!" he said.

I pushed past the iron gates and he said, 'It's like being in a CSI show, isn't it?" I just nodded. I was sweating from being rushed, carrying a bag of discarded ambulance material and blood-drenched sheets and clothing. I don't know what episodes of CSI he watched, but I definitely didn't look the part of the glamourous made-up forensic cleaner shown on TV. Police officers didn't usually sit in garden chairs reading newspapers in those shows either.

We were standing where the body had lain and he began to tell me what had happened.

"He was a known criminal," he said, "big guy. We'd been told he had firearms inside the property. His girlfriend let us in so we didn't need a warrant. He came home about ten minutes later, carrying on. He had a weapon and he chased my two officers and trapped one of them in the carport. My officer had no choice but to fire. He missed the first time!" As he was saying this, he pointed to the back fence and the house behind. "The bullet went through the fence into the house next door."

I was horrified to see a fence paling from the small house next door that had been blown away.

"The officer got him though!" he continued, as if shooting into the house next door was nothing. "Hit him twice in the lower part of his body, wounded him badly, he was still alive when the ambulance arrived. I've been told he is now deceased."

As he finished talking, I opened my mouth.

"It is like we're on CSI, isn't it. Funny thing is, you think you're the actor and I'm just the extra. But I get paid like the actor and you like the extra." He said no more. I laughed, we parted ways and I drove home.

Trailer Park Trash

You can drive past a landmark every day of your life and never take any notice of it. That is, until one day, something happens that makes you look at it every time you pass.

There was a rundown tourist caravan park on the main highway in the town where I lived. It had been there for as long as I had. Aside from scrunching up my nose at the pool, which regularly turned green from lack of maintenance, I never gave it a second look.

When I got the call for the job, I was happy to know it was close to home.

Oh, how I regret it now.

People living in caravan parks always used to make me think of the American term 'trailer trash'. But after having done various jobs in caravan parks, I had come to realise that they were more like a small community populated mainly by the elderly. Most of them were lonely, despite having neighbours less than two metres away.

This one was no different.

I pulled up alongside the caravan and laid my equipment on the grass. The curtains in the caravan were pulled closed across the sliding glass windows. Outside stood a BBQ.

I dressed in my white suit from head toe, and with gas mask in hand, thought that this wasn't something this little community would usually see. A man being taken away in a body bag, and then someone coming to clean up.

When people ask me questions about my profession after they hear my job title. The shock factor is what thrills me most. Growing up, I always tried to shock my parents. Even now, I get tattoos and recently had my septum pierced, just to see the reaction on people's faces. I love it.

The man had been dead for a week before anyone noticed the swarm of flies that was hovering towards the light shining through the gap in the curtains across the mould-covered windows. He had died in the winter, although it had been surprisingly hot. Heat makes a body decompose faster than normal. This was going to be bad.

The caravan was the size of my walk-in wardrobe, all boarded up and with the remains of a week-old decomposing body inside.

My best friend today would again be my gas mask.

Talking my last breath of fresh air before being confined to the gas mask for the rest of the afternoon, I pushed past the venetian blinds to a filthy mess. The tiny space was bursting with furniture and possessions. An unmade bunk bed against one wall was covered in clothing, with books on the floor beside it. Along the other wall was a kitchenette. Old dishes and food remains lay rotting in the sink and on the dining table. I noticed blood spots on the bed covers and edged closer to it. A dark patch of blood was smeared across the fake-wood floors. This was the beginning of the trail to what lay two feet away. Flies were everywhere and the more I perspired in my suit, the more they were attracted to me. The floor looked as if it was moving. As I reached what appeared to be a black curly wig on the floor next to the bed between the books,

I jumped back in horror. The ground was covered in maggots and what I had thought was a wig was the hair that had belonged to the man who once lived here. By this time in my career, I was used to the sight of a decomposing body, but a smelly, hairy, maggot-infested pile of mush made me feel sick. Without my mask, the smell would have made me vomit. I kept looking away as I began to wipe away what was once a grown man.

I have never researched the exact process of decomposition because I don't want to know. When I want a reaction from people, I explain that a decomposing body looks like a cooked shop-bought chicken with fat and liquid swirling around in the bottom of the bag. Leave it longer and it will begin to rot. Of course, it's something that people shouldn't have to see. It should happen underground.

The bodily fluids had spread all over the books and seeped under his bed. The books were soppy, as if they'd had tea poured over them, tea that was chunky and had maggots swimming in it. On my hands and knees, I mopped up his sloppy remains. I cleared a safe access area to the main site of contamination, as it was hazardous to my health and everyone else's. After that, I could remove all contaminated and porous items.

The bed had pools of stale blood on it. The pillowcase was smudged with blood and blood was soaked into the underlay. He had died of a heart attack. He'd been a heavy smoker so he may have been coughing up blood.

His girlfriend had been staying there with him. She had asked the managers if her sunglasses were in there. I kept wondering how she hadn't found him earlier. He would have been visible from the sliding door or through the window. Her boyfriend had dropped dead on the floor and she was worried about a pair of sunglasses. I did end up finding them and they weren't designer.

That's what I had expected, a pair of Dolce and Gabbana frames, but they were service station sunnies.

He seemed to have been a simple man, surrounded by books and old cassette tapes. He liked his cigarettes and didn't clean up after himself, and neither did his girlfriend.

I still drive past that caravan park every week and can't help myself from looking at it and at the green pool. I get a shiver down my spine every time and the sensation that maggots are crawling on the ground below my feet.

Daddy's Girl

I've always been a daddy's girl. My dad and I are similar in so many ways it always makes me smile. I'm proud to be just like him. Creative, street wise and sometimes a little naughty. I wouldn't want to be any other way, or have my dad be any different. I am blessed to have two beautiful parents who brought me up the best way they knew how. They showed me how exciting life can be and made sure I turned out to be respectful and good. Although not as well behaved as my sister. My parents aren't drunks, drug addicts or abusive.

There are a lot of children in this world who can't say the same.

I would have been categorised as a binge drinker, someone who drinks to get drunk, someone who doesn't have a sip all week but makes up for lost time on a Saturday night and well into the early hours of Sunday. I never realised how alcoholism affects the lives of those around you, until I saw grown men covered in their own vomit and faeces, dead from liver failure, and no one knowing they'd died until weeks later. People like this are used to smelling a foul odour coming from their own bodies from their lack of hygiene. They are used to having no money and living amongst filth and dirt.

Other alcoholics hide it well until they slip up and make silly decisions when they are intoxicated, leading to a trail of destruction.

The house was in a new area just south of Brisbane. The neighbourhood looked like a Monopoly board game, with all the houses matching except for the odd one in between that was bigger than the rest.

It was a refreshing change to work in a new property. It wasn't the usual run-down shack I was used to. I opened the front door and saw bloody footprints leading away from where I stood. They were perfect, like footsteps in freshly laid concrete. One trail of footprints led away from me and one towards me. The occupants of the house had left me the keys and they would meet me shortly on their way to work. They had been staying at a friend's house. It had been a break and enter, and the intruder had cut himself (or herself, I didn't know yet) badly upon entry. Starting at the doorway, I began removing the bloody footprints to make a safe entry and exit point for me. The last thing I wanted was to trudge blood throughout the house. Although the police had already been and assessed the site, I didn't want my footprints blending in with the intruder's.

Turning the corner, I was confronted by blood-soaked sheets on the carpeted lounge room floor. Bloody footprints continued onto other parts of the carpet.

This was a new rental property, but the carpets were soaked with blood, the grout in the kitchen and bathroom tiles was bloodstained, the window in the lounge room was smashed, the venetian blinds were bloodstained, as was the floor beneath them, and shards of glass were stuck in the floor. The only room that was untouched was the dining room. It looked as if nothing had been stolen, and nothing seemed out of place. The stereo system and TV were still there. I was confused.

I lifted the sheets and a pattern emerged. I didn't know if the intruder had survived. There was as much blood on the floor here as in any of the stabbing murders I had attended. After removing the sheets from the lounge room, I lifted those in the kitchen and the footprints revealed a bloody mess at the base of the fridge. The fridge door was smeared with blood and the inside was no different. The footsteps didn't continue further into the kitchen but went back out and turned down the hallway.

Like a game of snakes and ladders, the footprints led two steps forwards and one back. He had been very unsteady on his feet. I figured that he had come crashing through the window in the lounge room and although he was bleeding profusely, he'd continued weaving his way through the house. He'd been intoxicated, which made his blood thinner, and so the bleeding was very heavy. His bloody footprints told a tale of sheer desperation, marking out his entry, his deceitfulness and then his attempt to escape.

Whoever this was had only wanted one thing from inside the house and that was the alcoholic contents of the fridge. The kitchen bench showed signs of a party the night before. A half-eaten birthday cake, and party poppers that were popped all over the bench.

The night had definitely ended in a bang.

I had been on my hands and knees wiping away the blood of an unknown person when there was a knock at the door.

I was now also covered in blood, up the sleeves of my suit and all down the front of me. I needed to change my suit but I wouldn't have time before greeting whoever was at the door. I hoped they knew what had gone on inside this house as otherwise, I was going to shock them.

As I got closer to the door, I saw two police officers who looked as shocked at the sight of me as I was to see them. "Oh, you're the cleaner!" one of them said.

"Can I help you?" I asked.

"We were just driving past and thought we'd check on the place."

"So I'm guessing you haven't caught the guy?" I queried.

"Have you found anything that could be used in evidence?" the other asked.

"As far as I'm aware, this site has been cleared for cleaning and if I find anything, I will hand it in as I always do. I have a job to finish before the family comes back," I added. We stood there in silence while blood mixed with chemicals dripped from the sleeve of my suit during the awkward silence.

Soon after they left, there was another knock at the door. The owners had arrived. She was a petite girl, dressed professionally, with blonde shoulder-length hair. He was a boy racer, in his WRX with his tough guy attitude and backwards cap. He was her protector. He must have been feeling that he had failed in this, as he kept touching her. She was distraught and he couldn't do anything to change that. That was my job. I'm the one who makes things disappear as if they had never happened. I make them a distant memory.

They stood whispering in the corner of the room, oblivious to the fact that I could hear what they were saying. The intruder had been her dad!

I could not imagine a dad ever doing that. My dad would never do that.

She looked over at me with sadness in her eyes and a half smile on her lips. She asked me how much longer I would be, as the insurance company was due to inspect the property for damages. I told her that I wouldn't be much longer, but the more visitors I had the longer it would take. I needed to make sure I hadn't left any blood behind.

I still hadn't finished when the insurance representative arrived.

The couple told him about the night and said they did not know who had broken in.

The couple wanted the insurance to cover all the damaged items and then they just wanted to move out of the house. The memories inside these walls were now tainted forever.

With the last of the bloody water tipped out, I packed up, left, and made my way home.

I called Dad to tell him about my day, and to tell him I loved him.

The Godfather

He was known at the local watering hole as the Godfather. He drank there with his friends almost every day.

We've all joked about dying and what songs we want played at our funeral, where we want to be buried or where we want our ashes scattered. In my case, I hope to come back and haunt, not horror movie style, but just for a bit of fun, an eternity of fun. We make light of the situation and laugh about it and say, 'if I go, make sure you get rid of my stash of secrets under my bed or in my top drawer before you call anyone.'

The Godfather was no different.

His best mate met me at the terracotta brick home I had been called to clean in a sleepy suburb and let me in. His eyes were swollen and puffy.

"I have to be honest, I've taken something from the house," he said to me.

I raised a concerned eyebrow, wondering why he would tell me. I think he thought I was part of the police investigation. He quickly blurted out, "I already removed his porn from his room but I forgot to check one final drawer. He always told me, 'if I die unexpectedly, don't let them see my porn'."

It must be some collection, I thought. I walked with him to the front door and pushed it back, gesturing for him to go inside first. I knew from what I'd been told that there was no risk to this man by going inside.

I watched him as he packed the magazines into garbage bags, making sure it wasn't the man's life savings. Putting 'porn' on a report as to what the room contained wouldn't have been the dead man's wish, and I didn't intend to record it.

I asked his friend what had happened. I wasn't being nosy. I needed to know. The death of a person who dies of natural causes creates a different scene than a death caused by a gunshot, a knife, or bludgeoning. When someone dies of the body shutting down and giving up, blood and body fluids are released. Different equipment is needed on different jobs. Preparation is the key to a perfect clean.

When the Godfather didn't show to have a few beers with his buddies, they were concerned and went to his house as he wasn't answering his phone. When they pulled up outside his home and saw his car parked in the driveway with the doors locked, their worry increased.

Unable to enter the property, they looked through every window and saw him lying in a heap on the bathroom floor.

They called for police and paramedics but it was too late.

He had died of a heart attack and had bled out slowly from the wounds inflicted after falling on the hard terracotta tiles in the shower.

Any scenario to do with showers always reminds me of the scene in the movie 'Psycho', where blood is dripping down the drain. I'm so dramatic. It was nothing like that, although the scene replayed in my head and I kept looking over my shoulder, especially when the shower door closed with a creak when I was inside the recess.

Watching movies with blood and gore no longer affect me the way they should. I know the difference between what is staged and what is real.

He was so neat and tidy, it was a pleasure to see. His clothing was neatly folded and everything was in its place. The house had a homely feel and everything was perfectly positioned.

The only exception was the ashtrays full of cigarettes on the counter top and the stale smell of smoke in the air.

There was blood on the bed and the bedroom floor. The blood trail led from the bed into the bathroom and pooled in the shower, and vomit covered the toilet. His last moments had been slow and painful.

I removed the blood from the bedding and mattress. Sealy mattresses are no longer a joy for me to look at. They make me sweat. So well stitched and so full of padding that I couldn't tell what was mould or sweat or blood spotting, so I needed to be safe and cut out more than was probably necessary. I wanted to scream in frustration as it took so much time and energy, and I couldn't leave the mattress with biohazard waste on it. His mates, who were paying for the clean-up, had asked me to leave the mattress at the front door to save money. They had a perfectly good trailer and didn't want the expense of a skip.

On the carpet, I used my Stanley knife to cut away through to the underlay, checking that it was free of blood.

The pattern of blood on the bathroom floor showed that he was on his hands and knees, crawling from the toilet where he had vomited towards the shower, where he managed to get inside, close the glass door behind him, and lie down to rest on the floor, still bleeding.

When your time is up, it's up. How cruel and painful it can be. We have no say as to what happens at the end of the road.

However, the positive I took from this job was the discovery that great friends are as rare and precious as diamonds. They will stick by your side and have your back even if you aren't around to see it.

The Godfather's final moments took place only a couple of kilometres from where I was living at the time. Whenever I'm driving around the roundabout that leads to his street, a memory of the day I worked there always flashes into my mind.

He won't be forgotten, especially at the pub.

Privacy Protected

I had been living a relatively normal life for the past few months, as my crime scene work had dwindled, although the fire still burned brightly inside me.

Between my secret life, I had begun working a regular nine to five job to get back in touch with the normal working world. I needed to have discussions that didn't revolve solely around death. I had become obsessed with death. Not in a mass murderer way, I just had a fascination with it, and I needed to shift my focus to avoid becoming a strange character in society.

Then when my phone rang one day with my boss's name on the screen, my heart jumped. I was happy that they still thought of me.

The job was basic and quick, they informed me. The initial information was minimal and my point of contact was missing in action. All I knew was I had to be in north Brisbane before nine in the morning. I had an address, a name and a starting time.

I rang the woman who was my first point of contact multiple times and left multiple messages, hoping that she would call me back. She worked in a government department that helped the mentally disabled. I didn't hear back from her.

The building I arrived at the next day was on a quiet street with apartments all around, and parking was an issue. I parked illegally and put a sign on my windshield stating I was an emergency vehicle carrying biohazardous waste from a crime scene clean-up company. I left my number with instructions to call if I was inhibiting anyone. This was going to have to do until I could find a closer park. I had a lot of equipment to carry on my own.

I approached the front entrance with my arms full of cleaning gear and looked through the doors. No one. I called the woman again without success and swore under my breath that I had better things to do than wait for her. I dropped my equipment beside the door and knocked on it so forcefully that it would wake the dead. Pun intended. A small woman approached and unlocked the doors. She was the woman I had been waiting for.

The woman greeted me and I begin questioning her at the front door. I didn't know what had happened and where the incident was located. My health and safety must always be my first priority.

We had a brief chat and she told me that there was a lot of blood in the bathroom but it was an isolated area so it would be safe to enter without my protective gear. I went inside to confirm this for myself. She was right. I could see the door was sealed off and the environment around was clean and tidy. I would still be suiting up. It's not always about what you can see, but what you can't.

Once I had all my equipment at the glass front doors, I took out my camera, pulled on my suit and walked inside. Other people were in the office already, leisurely walking around, not even flinching that a stranger had walked into their domain covered from head to toe in protective clothing. In all other cases, no one must be on site when I am working, for their own safety and my insurance. This case was different. Because the incident had happened in a government building, it had to remain open.

Walking into the bathroom where the incident had happened, I blinked several times to see if what I was seeing was correct.

It looked like someone had cut their knee. There was hardly any blood. The bathroom was very bare. A stainless steel bin stood in the corner and a yellow needle disposal unit above that. I walked back into the main area and pulled out a blue plastic chair to write up my initial report. My contact came and sat down next to me.

I asked her, "Please tell me what happened here? I need this information for my report."

A known drug addict in the area had come into the building and gone into the bathroom, shooting up heroin in his arm. He hit a main artery and blood squirted from the pinprick he had made, which explained the blood pattern and smeared blood on the tiles. He thrashed about in the bathroom and somehow ended up outside on the footpath, overdosing. I asked for his name and the outcome of his episode. This was needed for my insurance as well as theirs.

I was taken aback when she said, "No," quickly following with, "I'm sorry, it's a closed case. His privacy is protected." I didn't say anything, but I thought that this man, in the hold of drugs, had gone into a public building, with no respect for anyone there, and selfishly exposed others to his blood and needles.

The clean-up took less than an hour. I removed all the blood, removed the needles and washed the bathroom down from ceiling to floor with disinfectant.

I left the room to dry and waited on the blue plastic chairs around the table in the center of the room before making a final inspection. A group of disabled people had just arrived, for either services or workshops being offered. They didn't ask why I was there, they just included me in their conversations about their favourite things, offering to share fruit from a bowl in the middle of the table with me, and smiling with joy as they selected clothes from a pile of second-hand donated items. I was a part of their world for those few moments, and I smiled along with them.

When it was time to go, I checked the bathroom again and then said goodbye to my new friends as I left.

Most of these people are shunned by society because they have something that is classed as 'not normal'. I have come to realise that no one is normal and that a smile and simple conversation warm the soul, even if the world is sometimes a cold, dark place.

Only the Lonely

I met a family member on the front steps of a pale pink house that looked to be from the 1990s. The front door was wide open and he was dressed in a polo and sandals. Before I could say anything, he opened the dusty screen door and invited me inside.

"Hold on a moment," I said, "I need to suit up! Do you have a mask or protective footwear?" I asked.

He looked at me, dazed and confused. "What could happen to me if I don't?" he responded.

I was yet to see inside, but there was a putrid stench wafting in the breeze. The smell is an indicator of gross filth, which is caused by bacteria, and in this case there was lots of it.

"From the smell alone you can get very sick!" I said.

His eyes widened. The family was hoping to stay for a few days to visit their grandmother, he said. She owned this home. I advised them not to, but I couldn't stop them. If they were trying to save money on a hotel, they would end up paying more on doctor's bills and antibiotics, I told him. As soon as I said that, he went into the garage and came back with gloves on, and then happily accepted the spare mask I held out to him. We walked inside and I was breathing very shallowly, and only through my mouth, even though I had the protective shield of my mask.

The house was large and decorated in trashy pale pink.

A pink chandelier hung in the foyer and another above the staircase. A large lounge area was off to the right and a hallway to the left. I took the pathway to the right and walked through the lounge room. It was very dirty and had nicotine-stained walls with a pink trim. There was a bar hidden somewhere under all the junk that was piled on top of it. Old food and cigarettes were hidden amongst everyday household items. Coffee cups were filled with a brown liquid that had chunks floating on the top. I couldn't work out what it had once been, flies or the congealing of its former substance. A once-pink floral printed couch against a banister was so heavily soiled it was a brownish-grey colour. Newspapers collected over years shared the second seat of the couch. I kept my opinions to myself as I walked around, with the family member close behind me. He and his whole family had been here many times before. This gross filth had accumulated over many years. He was not shocked.

I am always saddened how family members can let others live in a tip and do nothing about it until the time comes when they might inherit some of the assets. This house was a huge asset. It was a two-storey home and was twice the size of most. Situated on a canal, it had a large pool and spa.

The lounge room led into the kitchen. The fridge door was ajar and cockroaches by the hundreds were frozen to death on the base of the fridge and the freezer above it. The stovetop and kitchen sink were overflowing with old food and cutlery. A pot on the stove was covered in maggots and the contents inside made it look as if the stove was on. The liquid inside was bubbling and moving with all the newborn maggots inside. I wanted to vomit. There was a billiard room over the landing and the billiard table was hidden under piles of junk. The walls were covered in memorabilia of family members dating back to the early 1900s. Everything was nicotine-stained a yellowy-orange. In the bathrooms, the toilet was marked with faeces that overflowed onto the floor and was as hard as concrete. The showers were dusty and piled with junk. Not only did the house smell, but she must have also. She never bathed, or brushed her teeth or her hair.

Her bedroom walls were also stained dark yellow from nicotine and the blinds were in such poor condition they were useless for their purpose. Her bed had no sheets and a once-white doona and pillows were now brown. My dog wouldn't even sleep on that, I wouldn't let him, let alone a human. Glass sliding doors into the ensuite bathroom were the gateway to hell. The toilet hadn't been flushed in months; it was overflowing with faeces covered in toilet paper. I looked away in disgust. I couldn't take any more in. I didn't breathe the whole time I was in the room. Dust a centimetre thick covered every bathroom accessory and the shower was again filled with junk, along with the remains of a rubber bath mat that had disintegrated into pieces.

Upstairs the carpet was heavily marked, although the rooms were nowhere near as bad. The walls were a pale yellow, unlike the dark yellow of downstairs. Everything was in its place and the beds were made. It was as if I was in a different property. However, the stench reached upstairs, even if she herself hadn't been up here for years. She was eighty-five years old and unable to climb the stairs. Three more bedrooms led off the hallway and the end room had an amazing view of the river, with a jacuzzi in the ensuite covered in dust and the carcasses of cockroaches.

Photos of happier times lined the walls. The family was very well to do and had once lived a life full of dinner parties and drinks on the deck. She was now reduced to sitting alone for days on end on the heavily stained couch drinking her tea, forgetting it was there and making another. It was a sad sight, and one that so many elderly are faced with every day of their lives. She had once been houseproud and she refused to employ a cleaner, even though she had hundreds of thousands in the bank. Admitting you need help is hard. It took a moment of weakness, when her body gave way and she fell hard onto the floor and was surrounded in her own blood. If it hadn't been for the kindness of her neighbour, who noticed the silence and darkness in the home for a few days, she would have died there on the floor, alone.

Her family told me that she wouldn't be returning to the house and I never met her, as she was being cared for in a home. This chapter in her life had come to an end.

It took almost two weeks to clean up the mess that had taken years to make. The stained walls returned to white when the nicotine was washed from them. We gutted the house from top to bottom, tearing the carpets from their dusty edges. The pink chandelier remained as the only internal decorative item, sparkling with the light that could enter through the cleaned and clear windows. The couch was tossed into the trash with all the other appliances that were bacteria bombs.

When we left, the house echoed with emptiness. The family never did come to stay.

In the End

I have taken strength from those left behind in the wake of death and trauma. From the outside, they show the world they are ok, even though just under the surface they are riddled with pain and guilt.

'If only', is a phrase I have often heard mumbled. Nothing can change what happened.

From my experiences behind the blue and white chequered tape, I have become colder. My heart is hardened to the 'first world problems' of the people around me. I've learnt that reality and horror movies aren't so different from each other. Horror happens when lives end tragically.

Rest in Peace, all those beautiful souls who lost their lives.

This is my life.

Printed in Great Britain
by Amazon